RICKY TIMS'

Convergence

QUILTS

MYSTERIOUS,

MAGICAL,

EASY,

AND FUN

C&T PUBLISHING

Text and artwork ©2003 Ricky Tims

EDITOR-IN-CHIEF: Darra Williamson

EDITOR: Cyndy Lyle Rymer

TECHNICAL EDITOR: Sara Kate MacFarland

COPY EDITOR/PROOFREADER: Lee Jonsson/Joyce E. Lytle/
Eva Simoni Erb

COVER DESIGNER: Christina Jarumay

DESIGN DIRECTOR/BOOK DESIGNER: Rose Sheifer

ILLUSTRATOR: Kirstie L. McCormick

PRODUCTION ASSISTANT: Jeffery Carrillo

PHOTOGRAPHY: Quilt photography by John Bonath, Maddog
Studio, Denver, CO; Digital photos by Ricky Tims and
Justin Shults unless otherwise noted

Published by C&T Publishing, Inc., P.O. Box 1456,
Lafayette, California, 94549

FRONT COVER: Spirit of the Deep

BACK COVER: Project quilt from pages 33 and 57

Library of Congress Cataloging-in-Publication Data

Tims, Ricky.
 Ricky Tims' convergence quilts : mysterious, magical,
easy, and fun / Ricky Tims.
      p. cm.
Includes index.
  ISBN 1-57120-217-X (paper trade)
1. Patchwork—Patterns. 2. Strip quilting—Patterns.
3. Quilting.
I. Title: Convergence quilts. II. Title.
TT835.T524 2003
746.46'041—dc21
                            2003001242)

Printed in China
10 9 8

*This book is dedicated
to all who believe
that nothing is impossible.*

Acknowledgments

Thank you, Mom and Dad, for supporting me each time I
took the road less traveled, even though you lost sleep.

Thank you, Justin, for being the wind beneath my wings.

Thank you, Leslie, for being there at the start and
cheering me on.

This book is filled with inspired Convergence quilt
variations thanks to the generous support of over two
hundred quilters who submitted photos for the book.
My sincere thanks to these talented people for creating
beautiful work and sharing it.

A special thank you goes to the countless individuals—
teachers, leaders, friends, students, colleagues, and
family—who, over the years, have encouraged me
to pursue my dreams.

Contents

From Rags to Stitches

Mesquite trees and prickly pear cactus are abundant. The "pears" make a great jelly.

Do you know how much people like to talk about quilting? As soon as I mention that I am a quilter, I am immediately inundated with stories of Aunt Gertie or Grandma Goodson who made quilts a bazillion years ago. I've learned about siblings who became estranged when one got the heirloom quilt and one did not. I've learned that just about everybody has a quilt in the cedar chest made from bits of old dresses, shirts, or neckties. I'm still amazed when someone says to me, "You quilt? Goodness gracious, I don't know *anybody* who quilts anymore. Didn't that die out a long time ago?" By now I wish I'd told them I write mathematical equations for college textbooks, or regulate the chemical levels at a water treatment plant. (That usually steers the conversation elsewhere pretty quickly.) Instead, I launch into my lecture about how quilting is thriving. I try to explain that my quilts probably look a little bit different from Aunt Gertie's quilts, and do my best to be a good ambassador for quilters everywhere. It never fails that at some point during the conversation I'm asked: "What in the world made you start quilting?" Many of you may be asking the same question, so let's get to it right away.

An Oasis in the Prairie

My life began in the mesquite-glazed plains of the North Central Texas prairie. You won't find clear lakes, mountains, green pastures, Neiman Marcus, street mimes, theme parks, or a zoo (unless you count the llamas at the Nativity during the annual Christmas light display), but you will find oil, cattle, prickly pear cactus, rattlesnakes, rowdy cowboys, big trucks, big hair, a big blue bank, red dirt, red draws (beer and tomato juice), and lots of Red Man® chewing tobacco.

The "big blue bank" is a distinctive Wichita Falls landmark.

In Wichita Falls, you will also find what we native Wichitans affectionately call *The Falls*. Wichita Falls was a boomtown founded in 1882 on the banks of the Wichita River, near the site of a little five-foot waterfall. The amazing truth is that somewhere along the way the waterfall got lost. Maybe a flood or earthquake took it, I don't know. Anyway, the city fathers decided to create a new one so folks would stop asking about it. The new waterfall is a delightfully muddy, man-made cascade built on the scooped-out side of the river bluff with a cemetery situated on top. We're mighty proud of it!

In Wichita Falls there's culture (the symphony, ballet, theater, and an art museum), education (Midwestern State University), sports (high school football, of course), entertainment (The Texas Ranch Roundup), and lots of crepe myrtle! The crepe myrtle is the official flower of Wichita Falls, which should come as no surprise since it is about the only plant that can survive the "hotter-'n-hell" summers and "frozen-to-the-bone" winters. Speaking of hotter 'n hell, Wichita Falls is home to the world's largest bicycle ride, the Hotter 'n Hell 100, which is held each year in the month of (you guessed it!) August! If you're looking for a great place to visit with inspirational vistas, perfect climate, or remarkable national monuments, go somewhere else. But, if you're looking for a place that has down-to-earth folks, time-honored values, lots of Texas pride, and an eighteen-foot crepe myrtle statue, then you're gonna love my hometown.

Family Portrait, 1933. My grandpa, Riley Alfred Newsom, with my granny, Bertie Marie McWhorter (pictured here holding my mom, Billie Irene) and his first child, Albert (standing in front).

Let's Go Back, Way Back

My quilt story actually begins before I was born—when my grandpa bought my granny a 1955 Sears Kenmore sewing machine. Mind you, Granny having a brand-new, store-bought item in her home was a rarity. You see, Granny was a product of the Great Depression. She wore things until they wore out, and used things until they were used up. Many of Granny's household furnishings came from a place she called the *Kickapoo Exchange*. Now, the *Kickapoo Exchange* wasn't your typical, old-fashioned general store, with wood-plank floors, a pickle jar, and a canary in a corner cage. The *Kickapoo Exchange* was Granny's nickname for the local dump. Don't get me wrong. Granny wasn't too poor to buy what she wanted. She just happened to be a very frugal

person with a knack for making use of things that other folks found useless. On her visits to the *Kickapoo Exchange* she'd often find what she thought was a perfectly good piece of furniture that needed to be refinished or reupholstered. To this day I distinctly remember her assortment of upholstery tacks and a closet filled with her favorite upholstery fabric—Naugahyde.

Growing up, I spent a great deal of time with Granny and Grandpa in their house on Lake Kickapoo, a muddy-red, man-made lake not too far from Wichita Falls. Each day would begin with a hearty breakfast, featuring Granny's incredible homemade biscuits, gravy, sausage, and all sorts of canned jellies and jams. Before heading out to the garden, Granny always made sure I had plenty of protection from chiggers. Chiggers, as you may or may not know, climb up your legs and bite you in the most unfavorable places. So there I would be each morning, standing on the porch with my Buster Browns on my feet while Granny doused me from the waist down with kerosene. I didn't smell very rosy, but the chiggers left me alone. Afternoons were spent swimming and fishing, and life was grand! Each evening after supper I can remember Granny sitting at her Sears Kenmore sewing machine making a pillowcase, an apron, or mending something that wasn't quite ready for the *Kickapoo Exchange*.

My late uncle, Bob Patterson of Bowie, Texas, was a professional photographer. He took this photo of me as a baby.

The Falls on the river walk is the most popular tourist attraction in the county.

The "infamous" crepe myrtle statue in Wichita Falls, TX

A detail of one of Granny's corduroy, wool, and flannel quilts tied with embroidery floss

Sometimes Granny made quilts, but they weren't the Log Cabin, Double Wedding Ring, or Sunbonnet Sue sort. Her quilt blocks were made from odd-shaped pieces of fabric that included corduroy, wool, and flannel. In some cases, her batting was a reclaimed wool blanket from the Army Surplus store. Needless to say, these quilts had to be tied. I can remember helping her tie a corduroy quilt she made for me when I was ten years old. Try to imagine the weight of these monstrosities. I've often said that as kids, when we were put to bed, we were *put to bed*!

The hotter, the better: These crepe myrtle blossoms thrive in the North Central Texas heat.

Gone with the Wind

On April 10, 1979, Wichita Falls was hit by a massive tornado. The path of destruction was over thirteen miles long, and often more than a mile wide. Thousands of houses, including ours, were destroyed. During the months of rebuilding, it was decided that Granny

(now a widow and getting up in years) needed to leave the lake and move closer to family. The truth of the matter is, Granny was full of mischief, and Mom wanted to keep an eye on her. So while our house was being rebuilt, a new house for Granny was built across the street.

By 1991, twelve years had passed, and Granny was well settled into her new life in Wichita Falls; but at 83, the years seemed to be taking a toll on her mobility. She began walking with a cane, and rarely drove her car anymore. She got a phone call from a fellow by the name of Pete Hudgeons, an

I took this poor-quality Polaroid photo of our destroyed house the day following the tornado. Mom and Dad had only two months left on their mortgage.

87-year-old acquaintance whom she had not seen in years. Pete was living in Lubbock, Texas, a four-hour drive by car from Wichita Falls. That day, over the phone, he proposed to Granny—and she said yes! Even more astounding was how quickly her presumed frailty disappeared. She threw away her cane, found the keys to her car, and drove, that day, to Lubbock to find Pete.

When Mom got home from work, she noticed Granny's car was missing. After a few unsuccessful phone calls to locate her, panic set in. The phone rang. It was Granny. She explained that she had driven to Lubbock, and was just fine.

Although rarely used, Granny's old Kenmore remains in my quilting studio.

"What in the world are you doing in Lubbock?" Mom asked.

Granny replied, "Well, uh, maybe it would be best if your new papa told you."

The news took all of us by surprise. We encouraged her to take her time, but she quickly informed us that at her age there wasn't any time to wait. Granny and Pete were married in Wichita Falls exactly two weeks later.

When the minister asked, "Do you, Bertie Marie, take this man to be your lawfully wedded husband, to have and to hold from this day forward," she replied, "I do, I do, I *surely* do!"

There was no reception and no honeymoon—just dust, gravel, and the smell of burning rubber as the newlyweds sped off to Lubbock to revel in their newly married bliss. As the car disappeared from sight, my Aunt Jimmie looked at my mom and asked, "Billie, what in the world do you think they're gonna do?"

Mom cocked her head, raised her eyebrows, and retorted, "They better be playing cards or dominoes!"

When Granny moved to Lubbock, she took only what she needed: some clothes and her favorite pots and pans. We not only had to sell her house, but also had to sort through all her belongings. When Mom asked me if I wanted any of Granny's things, I took a mental inventory of her possessions and thought—*Kickapoo Exchange*. I suggested that Mom let the other family members take what they wanted. When all was said and done, I ended up with Granny's 1955 Sears Kenmore sewing machine.

A Stitch in Time: 1991

In June 1991, the sewing machine made the journey from Wichita Falls to my home in St. Louis, where it lurked in the corner of my dining room. Being the "Renaissance man" that I am, and having a little extra time on my hands (I was a "freelance" music producer—freelance being a fancy way of saying I was unemployed), I decided to make something. I decided to make a shirt. I thought, "Mama taught me to wind the bobbin, what more do I need to know?" Then I realized that a shirt might be too difficult, so I decided to make something a bit easier—a quilt. A quilt had to be easier than a shirt because it was flat—or supposed to be flat, if you know what I mean. I bought a book on sampler quilts and some fabric. In no time, I was hooked, and the rest is history.

This is one of the few photographs of Granny and Pete together. August 1993

Frequently Asked Questions

Q: What happened to Granny?
A: Granny passed away suddenly in November 1993 of a heart attack. She was eighty-five. She had two good years with Pete.

Q: Do you still use her sewing machine?
A: No, not on a regular basis. It is a good machine for piecing, but now it is simply a shrine in my sewing studio.

Q: Who quilts your quilts?
A: I do. Thank you very much.

Q: Do you quilt on a professional, longarm quilting machine?
A: No, I use a regular machine and quilt free-motion.

Q: How do you get a large quilt into that small space?
A: We're straying from the point of this book, but I will give you a few guidelines in Finishing Touches on page 73.

Nothing New Under the Sun

Do you, like me, find that when you think you have a new idea, you soon learn that someone else has already thought of it? When you think about it, most discoveries are made by accident. During elementary school many of us were taught that Christopher Columbus discovered America. The truth is, he bumped into it by accident while attempting to find a westward route to Asia. In 1929, Alexander Flemming discovered an unexpected fungal colony on an agar plate streaked with bacteria that had been left unattended for an unusual length of time. Flemming's curiosity about the fungus eventually led to the widespread production of an antibiotic that continues to save the lives of millions. The accidental discovery? Penicillin!

Flying Colors, Ricky Tims, 64" x 53", 1999

My Big "Accidental Discovery"

I discovered the guiding principles of Convergence quilts on my own. However, now that I'm tuned into this concept, I spot examples in the most unlikely places. I recently noticed a temperature control in an automobile that used a convergence of red and blue to indicate a mix of hot and cold air.

I'm sure that prior to my own "discovery," artists, mathematicians, and designers implemented the same principles in their work, so I don't have a personal claim. On the other hand, I enjoy exploring and developing convergences and variations of them. I also love to share these discoveries with fellow quilters.

I like to start a new project with a clear conscience. One day, while reorganizing my studio, I unearthed a set of Flying Geese blocks a group of quilters made for me. I stopped cleaning and began playing with the blocks. Suddenly a beautiful quilt began to emerge. I was lost in the creative process and the studio never did get clean. Sound familiar?

Flying Colors, back view

"What would happen
if the strips were cut
in graduated widths?"
and "What would
happen if they were
then sorted into
each other?"

I sewed the top together, and I decided to finish it for a local quilt show. I chose two hand-dyed spirals to use on the back, but when I laid them side by side, they looked like two dizzy owl's eyes. I thought about slicing them into strips and rearranging them, but before I did other questions came to mind.

After slicing, converging, and sorting the two spirals, I realized they were too big for the back, so I had to remove about ten inches from each spiral. The back of *Flying Colors* is shown above.

The result was amazing! I considered other possibilities such as: "What would happen if, after the first set of strips were converged and sewn vertically, they were then cut and converged horizontally?" I pursued my experiment with a single piece of multicolored, hand-dyed fabric that I cut into four squares. The result of that experiment was a quilt I named *Genesis*, which means beginnings.

Harmonic Convergence I: Genesis, Ricky Tims, 32" x 33", 1999. The interior of this quilt was made from a single fabric. The quilt was machine quilted with a flame stitch (see page 74) using two variegated rayon threads in a single needle.

Harmonic Convergence II: Firestorm, Ricky Tims, 30" x 30", 1999

My project names often have a musical reference; so, in trying to come up with a name for this method I chose "Harmonic Convergence." I loved the way the fabrics and colors harmonized as they were converged, so the name Harmonic Convergence seemed appropriate.

There is nothing new under the sun! I recently learned about a mystic "new age" group who believe that a prophetic New Age of Peace, the Harmonic Convergence, began on August 17, 1987.

My Harmonic Convergence quilts are not related to that movement, and if the name is too difficult to remember, you are welcome to follow the example of a student in the U.K. who stood up at show-and-tell with her Harmonic Convergence quilt. Having forgotten what it was called, she said, "I took Ricky's workshop yesterday and this is my version of his...ahm...ahh...Colonic Irrigation!" Sometimes I call it Ricky Tims' Strip Tease. When I do, the class registrations skyrocket! Call it what you like. Just have fun!

I was both pleased and surprised with the results of *Genesis*. Thinking that it might have been a fluke, I tried the process again with another single piece of hand-dyed fabric. The result of the second experiment is called *Harmonic Convergence II: Firestorm*.

After the second experiment, I was convinced that the process would work in a variety of ways. I used two spirals on the back of *Flying Colors*, but was curious to see what would happen if I used just one spiral to make a Harmonic Convergence quilt. I began with a spiral about 44" square and divided it into four 22" squares. Then I followed the same steps I used in the previous two quilts. When *Harmonic Convergence III: Circle of Life* was complete, I was amazed to see the original design of the spiral intact.

I revisited the back of *Flying Colors*. Even though it was only converged vertically, the effect was successful because of the interaction between the two designs. I tried another experiment. This time I layered two squares and cut them simultaneously with two diagonal swoops. I exchanged the center pieces in the blocks, then sewed the blocks back together. Finally, I sliced the two blocks into strips and converged them vertically. *Divide and Conquer: Awakening* was the final result.

Harmonic Convergence III: Circle of Life, Ricky Tims, 36" x 38", 1999

Divide and Conquer: Awakening, Ricky Tims, 41" x 23", 1999

Divide and Conquer: Lava Flow, Ricky Tims, 42" x 25", 1999

Not being one to trust the results of one experiment, I had to try just one more time. I layered two squares, cut two gentle diagonal curves, sewed the blocks back together, and converged them. This time I wasn't as pleased with the result; the design seemed weak. Brainstorm! When I brought the design out into the border, it was much stronger. Lesson learned: Borders can really impact the overall design.

Until now, I had cut all the strips in graduated widths. It was time to see what would happen if I cut the strips in equal widths. I chose two multicolored fabrics that already had a strong surface design. I cut the two fabrics into strips of equal width, then converged the strips. It dawned on me that since all the strips were even widths, I could cut horizontal strips and shift every other strip left or right, creating a sort of checkerboard effect. Another ah-ha! I could take out a strip, turn it 180°, and insert it near the bottom. Another success! This one is called *Skyfire*.

As you can see, one experiment led to another. I was excited about the checkerboard effect in *Skyfire*, and wanted to see what would happen if a single fabric was made into squares. I cut vertical strips of equal size (in width and length) and sewed them back together without rearranging them. Then I cut horizontal strips of equal size and shifted every other row over one square. The interior of *Misty Morning* has the effect of a colorwash quilt, but is made from only one fabric.

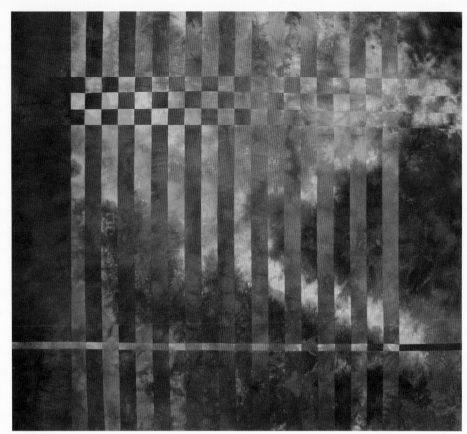

Skyfire, Ricky Tims, 46" x 38", 1999

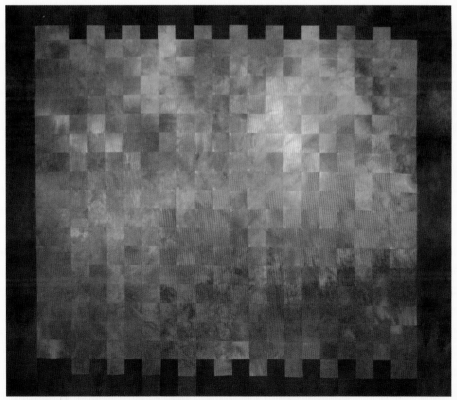

Misty Morning, Ricky Tims, 43" x 34", 1999

Untitled, Ricky Tims, 36" x 18", 1999

Remember how I had lopped off the ends of the original spiral that I used on the back of *Flying Colors*? Well, I decided to use them in a way similar to the method used in *Misty Morning*. I cut both fabrics into strips and sewed them together without converging them. Then I sliced them horizontally and shifted each row over one square. The result was *Untitled* on this page.

I tried another experiment. I decided to create a quilt panel that had set-in concentric circles and a few flowing curves. I drew the design on freezer paper and cut it apart to create templates. After sewing the panel together, I sliced it into even-width strips. Then I took a single multicolored fabric and sliced it into strips of various sizes. Starting in the center of the fabric, I began to slice narrow strips that got wider as they moved out toward the edge. I converged this set of strips

from the panel with the strips from the single piece of fabric. Lo and behold, I ended up with *Bi-Polar Solar System* on page 15.

The previous examples show the development of Convergence quilts. There are many variations of Convergence quilts yet to be explored. You may notice that only two of them are quilted. Each quilt played a role in leading to the next experiment. At the time, my enthusiastic search for answers was more important than quilting the quilt. These are the quilts that answered my questions, and led to many more completed quilts.

While I like to use my own hand-dyed fabrics, the galleries are filled with many beautiful quilts made by my students and others who have used a variety of fabrics. I am confident these quilts will inspire you to create your own exciting Convergence quilt.

The Nitty Gritty of Convergence Quilts

In my experience, the most successful way to learn is to move past idle curiosity to actual exploration and experimentation. Convergence quilts go together fairly quickly, so you won't have wasted a lot of time exploring an idea, or used too much of your favorite fabric if you aren't exactly thrilled with the results. The process will teach you something, if nothing more than, "Well, I won't do that again." On the other hand, you may create something new, original, and perhaps even more exciting than you had hoped for or imagined. Once you understand the guidelines for Convergence quilts, you may begin asking:

"What would happen if...?"

Bi-Polar Solar System, Ricky Tims, 41" x 39", 1999

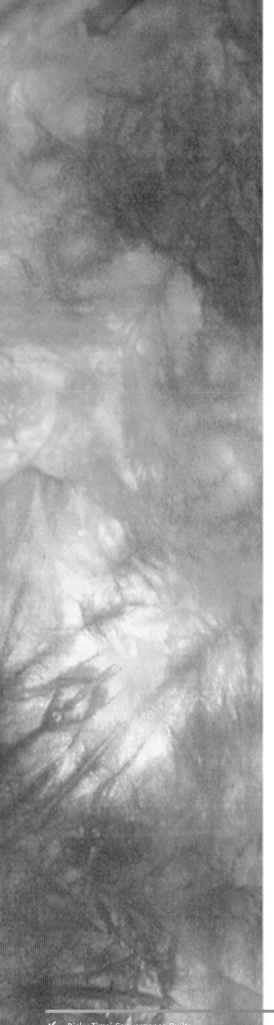

What *Is* a Convergence Quilt?

A Convergence quilt features two or more designs that are cut into strips and then merged together. I don't usually rearrange or invert the strips before converging them. I prefer to keep them in order because I like to see the design flow through the convergence. However, there is nothing wrong with inverting or rearranging the strips to see what happens. Some quilters like what happens to the design when random strips become inverted. There are no rules for Convergence quilts, but there are some guidelines that should help you create successful designs.

Design Origins

A Convergence quilt begins with a design source. The designs may be printed or dyed directly on the fabric (wholecloth), made from several fabrics (pieced, appliquéd, or both), or created by converging a wholecloth design with a constructed design. In addition, the widths of the strips can be cut incrementally, evenly, randomly, or by combining any of these options. The overall effect can be vertical, horizontal, or both. You can also create a diagonal convergence (see pages 18 and 19).

Slicing and Dicing

There are many ways to slice fabric into strips. Take time to become familiar with the various options presented below.

In order to help you understand the process, I consistently defined each type of division by the position of the narrowest strip(s).

EDGE GRADATION

In an edge gradation, you cut a fabric or a design into strips beginning on one side. As you cut, each subsequent strip gets wider as you move toward the opposite side. Edge gradations can be right to left, left to right, bottom to top, or top to bottom.

NOTE: The exercises in this book focus on vertical and horizontal convergences, but a few of the gallery quilts show that diagonal convergences can also be successful.

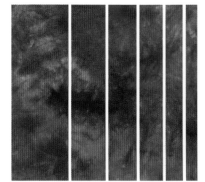

A right-edge gradation (cut from right to left)

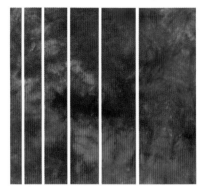

A left-edge gradation (cut from left to right)

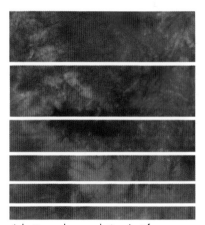

A bottom-edge gradation (cut from the bottom up)

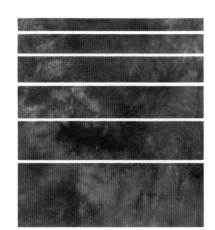

A top-edge gradation (cut from the top down)

INSIDE-OUT GRADATION

For an inside-out gradation, you cut the fabric from the center out. The narrowest strip(s) are in the center, and subsequent strips get incrementally wider as you move toward the edges. An inside-out gradation with an odd number of strips features one narrow strip in the center; two strips in the center yields an even number of strips.

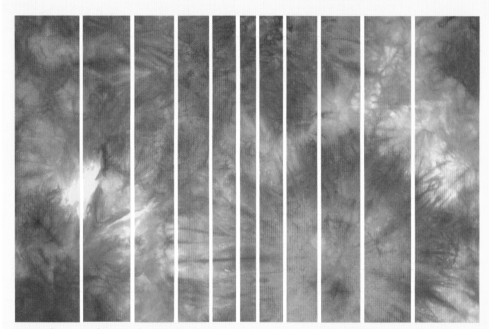

An inside-out gradation with 11 strips

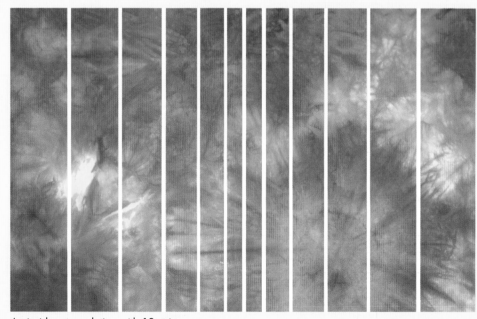

An inside-out gradation with 12 strips

OUTSIDE-IN GRADATION

For an outside-in gradation, you cut the strips in graduated widths from both sides. The narrowest strips are at the sides, and each subsequent strip gets incrementally wider as you move toward the center. Again, one strip in the center leads to an odd number of strips; two strips in the center yields an even number of strips.

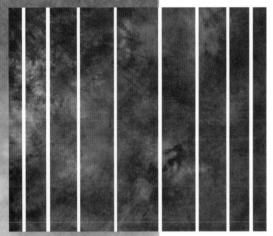

An outside-in gradation with 9 strips

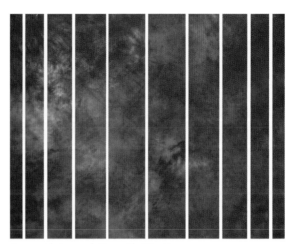

An outside-in gradation with 10 strips

SPACER STRIPS

Fabrics or designs cut into strips of equal width, regardless of the measurement, are considered spacer strips. Spacer strips can be used vertically, horizontally, or diagonally.

Vertical spacer strips

Diagonal spacer strips

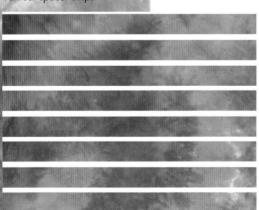

Horizontal spacer strips

RANDOM STRIPS

As the name implies, fabrics or designs cut into strips of random-size widths are called random strips. Random strips can also be used vertically, horizontally, or diagonally.

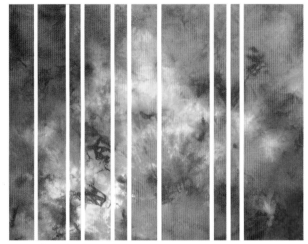

Vertical random strips

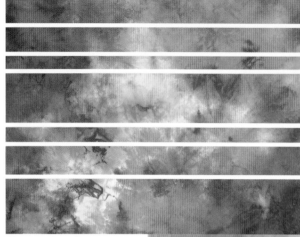

Horizontal random strips

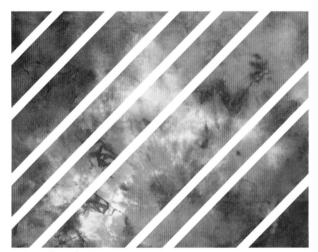

Diagonal random strips

When cutting a sequence of graduated strips, it is best to stop the sequence if the remaining strip of fabric would be smaller than the previous strip. I prefer to leave the final strip wider than necessary, instead of trimming it to the next incremental width. I can always trim it later, when I square the quilt before adding borders.

Strip Width Options

When I slice the fabric into strips, I prefer to cut in $1/2$" increments. For example, for a right edge gradation I first cut a 1" strip on the right edge of the fabric. Subsequent strips are cut in widths of $1^{1}/_{2}$", 2", $2^{1}/_{2}$", 3", and so on. These measurements are the unfinished-size strip widths. Naturally, the strips will be narrower when sewn together.

It is certainly possible to use $1/4$" increments rather than $1/2$" increments, especially when creating a miniature Convergence quilt. In reality, *any* strip width is possible, and the measurement options allow for infinite Convergence quilt variations.

What About Fibonacci?

Fibona…what? Fibona…who? Leonardo Pisano, better known by his nickname, Fibonacci (fih-bo-*nah*-chee),was a famous mathematician born in Pisa, Italy around 1170. One of his surviving theories is a formula known as the Fibonacci Numbers or Fibonacci Sequence, which states that the current number is the sum of the two previous numbers, where the first two numbers are equal to one (that is, the first eight Fibonacci Numbers are 1, 1, 2, 3, 5, 8, 13, 21). In other words, 1+1=2, 1+2=3, 2+3=5, 3+5=8, and so on.

I've included this section on Fibonacci because I am often asked if the Fibonacci Sequence will work when cutting strips for a Convergence quilt. My usual answer is, "Try it and see!" Having said that, I find that by using this sequence, the strip widths increase very fast—a result that could be good or bad. The sequence does not have to begin with 1" strips. Consider starting with ½" strips. The sequence would then be ½", ½", 1", 1½", 2½", 4", and so on. I also recommend that when using this formula the first repeated number (the first ½") be omitted. This sequence keeps the strips from getting too wide too fast. Using the Fibonacci Sequence is a viable option for cutting strips. Experiment! You just might like the results.

Visualizing a Convergence

In most cases, I recommend that Convergence quilts be treated as "mystery" quilts. In other words, don't over-plan, and don't worry if you can't visualize the final result. Allow the excitement to unfold as you progress through the project. Having said that, the following photos will help you understand what happens to a fabric or a design when it is dissected. By showing the designs alone—dissected, but not converged with other fabrics or designs—you will get an idea of how a fabric may be positioned within a convergence. The effect will be dramatically different when the strips from this first fabric are converged with other fabrics or designs.

VISUALIZING VERTICAL AND HORIZONTAL CONVERGENCE

The photos below show how a single square of multicolored fabric (wholecloth) can be cut in a variety of ways. In an Original Harmonic Convergence quilt, strips are cut in graduated increments both vertically and horizontally.

As you will see on page 28, in a Harmonic Convergence quilt, this fabric would have been Fabric #1, in the top-left corner.

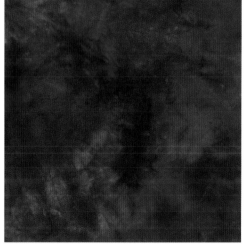

A single 15" square of multicolored fabric

Right edge and bottom edge gradations combined

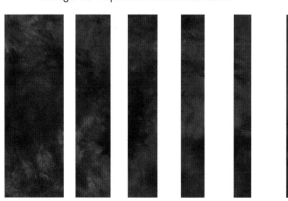

The same square dissected using a right edge gradation.

Cut a square so the focal point image
(the fish) is in a corner.

Good placement

In the example above, I separated and expanded the design vertically, horizontally, and diagonally. I also expanded the space between the pieces incrementally.

The first photo shows a single fabric before it was converged with another fabric or design. Refer back to this photo to help you understand the actual distribution of the fabric in a final convergence.

You can see what happens to the square when it is in the upper-left corner (the position of Fabric #1 in Harmonic Convergence). When the strips are cut, the design divides and expands, but the fish remains dominant in the design.

Notice what happens if the same square is placed in the bottom-right corner of a Harmonic Convergence. The focal point, the fish, now dissipated, becomes lost in the overall design.

VISUALIZING SINGLE DIRECTION CONVERGENCE

When planning a single direction convergence, try to use designs that oppose the direction of the strips. For example, if you are planning a vertical strip convergence, try to use a design that is horizontal or diagonal. (If you choose or create a design that is primarily vertical and then proceed to dissect it vertically as well, the overall effect will be lost when it is converged.)

Poor placement

A block with a strong swooping
horizontal and diagonal flow

Sliced and expanded, the design remains strong.

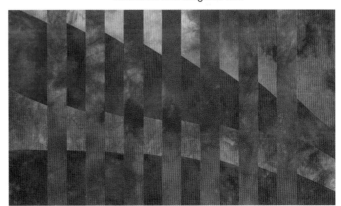

The design is converged with another fabric and the flow
remains prominent.

In the photo at left, the same pieced square is turned, and the design is now vertical and horizontal. In this position, the design will lose its strength when converged with another fabric.

In the next photo, the overall design is less effective because of the similarity of the vertical piecing and vertical strips. The right diagonal corner is the only part of the quilt that still has any impact.

The square is turned.

When cut and expanded, the design is weaker.

Making your fabric and design choices is a lot of fun. Remember, you cannot fully visualize what will happen with each quilt, but that's part of the fun. This chapter has not exhausted the possibilities, but by getting acquainted with the principles behind Convergence quilts, you will see what effects certain convergences create, and may even create something totally new.

Gradation Possibilities Summed Up

You can start a gradation from any area you choose. Here is a review of just some of the possibilities:

1. Left edge
2. Right edge
3. Bottom edge
4. Top edge
5. Inside out
6. Outside in

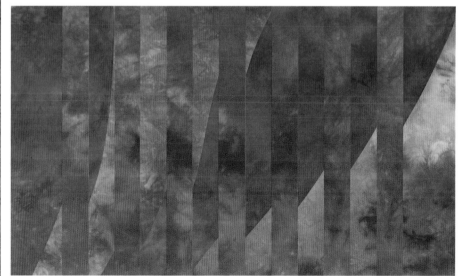

Poor design choice

General Tips and Guidelines

Choosing Fabrics

Have you ever purchased an expensive, beautiful, one-of-a-kind hand-dyed fabric just so you could take it home to pet and fondle every now and then? Many quilters have experimented with dyeing, but are reluctant to use their one-of-a-kind fabrics because it seems such a shame to cut it into pieces. When I began experimenting with convergence, I felt the same way. At first, I always reached for my least favorite pieces. I wasn't about to use the good stuff! Sound familiar? I only used fabric that was "expendable" or deemed appropriate for experimentation. Well, even when I used the "ugly" fabrics, the results were amazing. With each experiment I became more and more excited, because the original beauty and integrity of the fabric was preserved. I had found a way to effectively use my own hand-dyed fabrics.

Although I make Convergence quilts from my own fabrics, many commercial fabrics can be used successfully in a project. Here are examples of fabrics that are excellent for making Convergence quilts.

MULTICOLORED HAND-DYED FABRICS

Stop petting your beautiful hand-dyed fabrics and use them in a Convergence quilt! The results will be spectacular and you will preserve the integrity of the beautiful, one-of-a-kind fabric. Multicolored, hand-dyed fabrics are beautiful when used exclusively in a quilt, but also provide excellent opportunities for color blending when used with commercial fabrics. To purchase fabrics like this, see page 79.

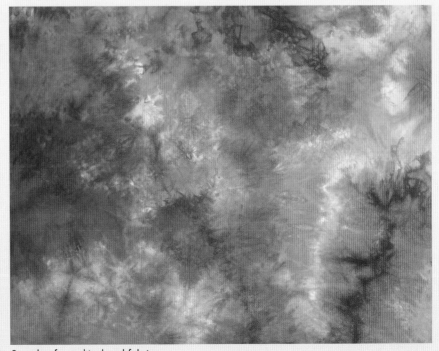

Sample of a multicolored fabric

Commercial Fabrics

Every fabric in a quilt shop can find a home in a Convergence quilt. Following is a sampling of various prints that tend to be successful with this method.

LARGE-SCALE PRINTS

Each of these fabrics is approximately a 16" square. In general, when you use a large-scale print, I suggest complementing it with smaller-scale prints or solids. Multiple large-scale prints tend to fight each other, and the final result is oftentimes visually distracting or confusing.

 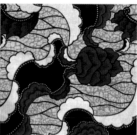 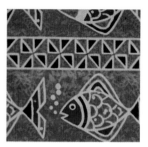

MEDIUM-SCALE PRINTS

These medium-scale prints provide texture and variety. Each of them can be effective when coordinated with other fabrics. However, they will maintain an overall sameness in a project.

DIRECTIONAL PRINTS

Don't be afraid to try directional prints. Even stripes can work with the linear aspect of a Convergence quilt to give it added punch. When you use a directional print, be sure to consider whether you want vertical/active lines or horizontal/passive lines.

  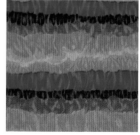

SMALL-SCALE PRINTS AND SOLID FABRICS

Many fabrics read as a solid color but, in fact, are really a print. An honest-to-goodness solid fabric will read the same as these fabrics that have a single, overall color or small-scale print. These fabrics will provide a distinct, one-color area throughout the quilt. Be sure to search the galleries for quilts in which solid or small-scale print fabrics were used.

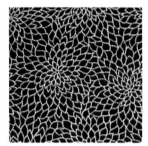 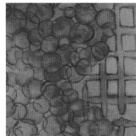 

You can create a beautiful Convergence quilt with just about any fabric. You just have to let the magic unfold.

Prewashing Fabrics

I suggest you prewash your fabrics before using them in a project. I primarily use my own hand-dyed fabrics that have been through a hot wash in Synthropol and two rinse cycles. When I do use commercial fabrics for my Convergence quilts, I prewash them, use spray starch or sizing, and press before cutting the strips.

Pre-starching Fabrics

As mentioned previously, I find that pre-starching your fabric for Convergence projects improves workmanship. Pre-starching helps keep seams straight and seam allowances accurate, and it helps prevent the bowing that often occurs when long strips are sewn together. Before you cut any strips, use spray starch and press. To prevent flaking, let the starch thoroughly soak into your fabric before pressing. You can also use liquid starch and follow the manufacturer's directions for a medium-starch treatment.

Accuracy

You might be happy to know that I am not a member of the quilt police. It is more important for me that you enjoy making Convergence quilts, and that you don't stress or fuss over a crooked or mismatched seam. We all sew at different levels of expertise, and we all experience growing pains as we learn new techniques and methods. Don't beat yourself up if your work is not at the same level as some well-known, prize-winning quilter. Having said that, as you progress you will naturally want to improve the quality of your workmanship. Better workmanship and accuracy are the result of three elements: careful or precise cutting, sewing, and pressing.

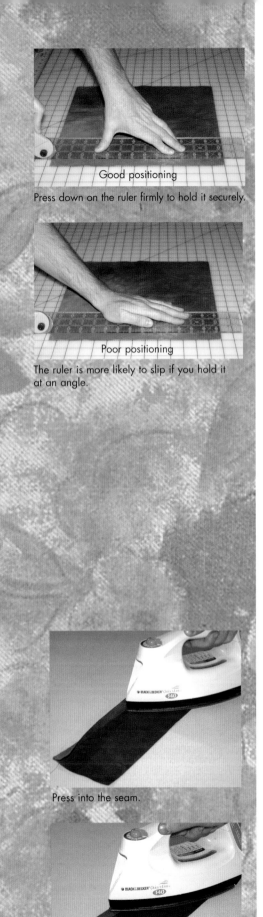

Good positioning

Press down on the ruler firmly to hold it securely.

Poor positioning

The ruler is more likely to slip if you hold it at an angle.

Press into the seam.

Press the seam flat.

CUTTING

Precise sewing begins with accurate cutting; accurate cutting begins with a good mat and a sharp rotary cutter blade. Nicks in the blade create frustration and diminish the quality of your cutting. If your blade gets a nick or becomes dull, replace it before continuing with your project.

The lines that are printed on mats and rulers are there to help you. Take time to properly align and firmly hold the ruler as you make each cut. The best advice I can offer is to be consistent with positioning when placing the ruler on mat lines or fabric edges. When you hold the ruler, put weight directly down onto it. The ruler is less likely to slip if you press down on it, instead of holding it at an angle. **Always cut by pushing the blade away from you. Never pull the blade toward you.**

SEWING

Good workmanship is also a result of precise sewing. It is important to make consistent seam allowances. Seam allowances for Convergence quilts *do not* have to be ¼". In fact, I recommend that you use a smaller than ¼" seam allowance. A smaller seam allows more of the beautiful fabric to remain on the surface, rather than being lost in the seams. Convergence quilt seams are sewn at right angles (except for improvisational curves,

Move the needle position to the right for smaller seams.

which are discussed on page 42), so they will fit together precisely and accurately as long as all the seam allowances are consistent.

To make smaller seams, I use a standard foot (instead of a ¼" foot) and move the needle position to the right. This smaller seam is sufficient for a secure seam. By using the right edge of the foot as a guide, you will make seams that are small and consistent. Be sure the edges of the two fabrics are lined up perfectly. The bottom fabric often slips to the left and becomes hidden under the top fabric. If the edges are not aligned, your strips will not be accurate, straight, and even. Avoid this problem by making sure you can always see a hairline of the bottom strip. Keep both edges accurately lined up with the right edge of the foot. Pre-starched fabrics are easier to align.

PRESSING

Never underestimate the importance of pressing to improve accuracy and workmanship. I recommend that each seam be pressed as soon as it is completed. Position the strips so one strip is right side up on the ironing mat. Hold the other strip up so it will fall away from you as you press. Inching down the seams, press from the right side of the fabric into the seam to assure a tight seam. Once the seam is tight, press the entire strip flat. If you wish, you can flip it over and press again from the wrong side. Pressing from the wrong side first may create pleats at the seam. Any additional pressing to remove pleats may cause distortion, which results in wavy or inaccurate patchwork.

There are many ways to achieve good workmanship. The methods I use may be different from the ones you prefer. If you find your methods work better for you, then, by all means, continue to use them. The guidelines I present in this book work well for me, and I hope they add to the success of your projects as well.

Original Harmonic Convergence

The Original Harmonic Convergence quilt design is popular for many reasons. In addition to being quick, easy, and fun, it is also a great project for both beginning and experienced quilters. I strongly recommend that before starting this project, you read through all of the steps and become familiar with the process. Pay particular attention to the special notes. They help with common concerns, and provide you with confidence and reassurance that you are on the right track. They also offer tips that can add to the success of your project.

Basic Supplies

You will need four same-sized squares of fabrics, a rotary cutter and large mat, fabric markers, and, of course, a sewing machine in good working order.

Fabric Selection

The four squares can range from 14"–16". When using commercial fabrics, choose four fabrics that coordinate. Consider a large print (tropical, oriental, floral, and so on) as one of your fabric choices. Another option would be to cut four squares from only two fabrics, and position them like a big four-patch. When you use multicolored hand-dyed fabrics, all four squares may be cut from the same fabric. The examples that follow feature a single piece of multicolored fabric.

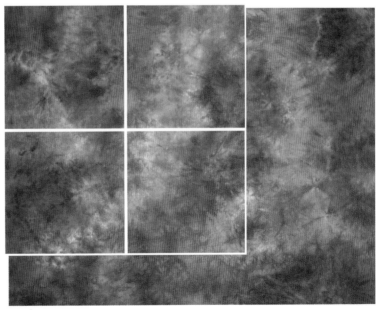

Cut four squares.

Steps for an Original Harmonic Convergence

Create a large four-patch, positioning the fabrics as desired.

FABRIC POSITIONING GUIDELINES

Because fabric choices for this project vary dramatically, it is impossible to give exact instructions as to how you should position your fabrics. The following guidelines will help you decide how to position your four squares. Use the suggestion that best fits your fabric choices.

• **If you choose a large-scale print**, put it in either the bottom-left or bottom-right corner, especially if it features animals, trees, flowers, and so on. The bottom position gives the appearance that the large elements are in the foreground, creating a sort of pictorial perspective. Make sure the printed image is not on its side or upside down.

• **If you have pairs of similar colors**, such as two blues and two oranges, place them diagonally across from each other. If you place them next to each other, either horizontally or vertically, the final convergence will have a striped appearance.

• **If you have a variety of colors**, place the two darkest and two lightest diagonally across from each other. As mentioned before, the diagonal four-patch positioning creates the best illusion.

• **If you are using multi-colored hand-dyed or multicolored commercial fabrics with large patches of color**, refer to Visualizing the Convergence on page 20 to help you determine the positioning. It will take some experience for you to fully understand how the colors will blend. Even then, remember that Harmonic Convergence quilts are a bit of a mystery, and part of the fun is letting the magic happen on its own. With multicolored fabrics you will rarely be disappointed, no matter what positioning you select.

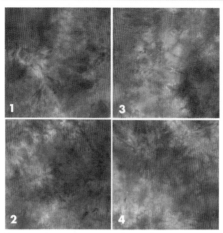

Position the squares as indicated.

1. Using a fabric marking pencil or pen, mark a line ¼" or less away from the top edge of Fabrics 1 and 3. This line will serve as an orientation guide throughout the project.

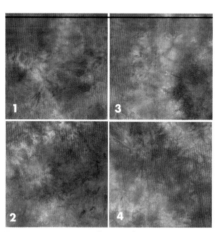

Orientation line

Draw an orientation line at the top.

2. Create a left unit and a right unit by folding Fabric 2 *up* onto Fabric 1, so they are positioned right sides together. (Do not fold Fabric 1 *down* onto Fabric 2). Use one pin to mark this bottom edge, so when you pick the fabrics up to sew, you will not accidentally sew along the wrong side. Sew the seam.

Repeat by folding Fabric 4 up onto Fabric 3 and sewing across the bottom.

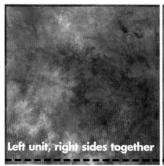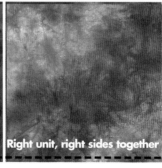

Left unit, right sides together   Right unit, right sides together

Sew along the bottom edge.

3. **Do not unfold the squares.**

   Referring to the photo, position the left unit on the cutting mat with Fabric 2 wrong side up and the sewn seam at the bottom. If the right edges are not perfectly aligned, make a fresh trim on the right edge before cutting the strips. Use the Strip Measurement Chart below to cut the unit into strips. Here the unit will be cut with a right edge gradation (right to left).

   Repeat the process with the right unit. If the left edges are not perfectly aligned, make a fresh trim on the left edge before cutting the strips. Use the Strip Measurement Chart below to cut the unit into strips. This time the unit will be cut with a left edge gradation (left to right).

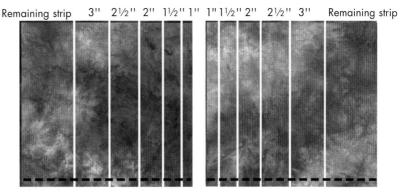

Remaining strip 3" 2½" 2" 1½" 1"   1" 1½" 2" 2½" 3" Remaining strip

Cut both units as indicated.

4. Unfold the strips so they are back in their original position with each unit side by side. The two narrowest strips should be next to each other in the center. Check to see that the orientation line is still across the top of all the strips. If a line does not appear at the top, look at the bottom. If it is at the bottom, invert the strip so the orientation line is at the top.

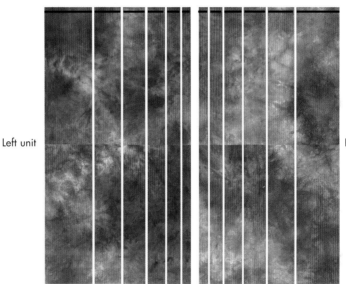

Left unit   Right unit

Unfold strips.

5. The strips from the left unit are merged with the strips of the right unit. Begin by moving Strip 1 of the left unit over between Strips 5 and 6 of the right unit.

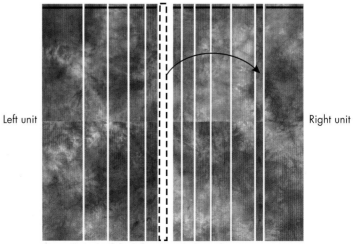

Left unit   Right unit

Move Strip 1 of the left unit as indicated.

STRIP MEASUREMENT CHART	
Strip 1	1"
Strip 2	1½"
Strip 3	2"
Strip 4	2½"
Strip 5	3"
Strip 6	remaining width*

* The width of this final strip is determined by the size of your original squares. The larger the square, the wider this strip will be. Do not toss the strip aside; it is Strip 6 and will be converged along with the other strips.

6. Move Strip 2 of the left unit between Strips 4 and 5 of the right unit. The strips of the right unit shift to make room for the new strips from the left unit.

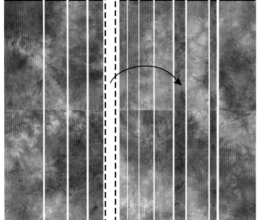

Left unit   Right unit

Move Strip 2 of the left unit as indicated.

7. Continue the sequence of moving the strips from the left unit between the strips of the right unit. As the right unit shifts left to make room for each new strip, the strips of the right unit will automatically end up in the correct position. If you have a design wall in your sewing room, place the converged strips on it. Number the converged strips 1 through 12.

1   2   3   4   5   6   7   8   9   10 11   12

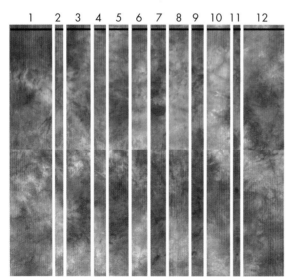

The strips are converged but not sewn together.

8. Once again, check to see that the orientation line is at the top of each strip. If any lines are at the bottom, you have inverted some strips. Position the strips so the orientation lines are at the top of each strip.

9. Halfway down each strip is a seam. Alternating up, then down, finger-press each seam. Sew the strips from top to bottom in pairs: sew 1 to 2, 3 to 4, 5 to 6, and so on. (See Tip 1 on page 31.) Work from the left to the right, matching the seams. (See Tip 2 on page 31.) Press all seams in the same direction.

10. Time to sew the pairs together. I recommend you sew them from bottom to top, which helps prevent bowing. Working from left to right, sew the pairs together, matching the single center seam on each pair. After each seam is sewn, place the unit back into the design. Confirm the strips are still in the correct position. Make sure the seams are all pressed in the same direction. Congratulations! You have completed the first half of your Harmonic Convergence quilt. It's time to celebrate. Take a break. Admire your work. Treat yourself to a slice of chocolate cake!

11. Turn the quilt a quarter turn to the left or right; either direction is fine. The strips will now be horizontal. This new orientation is only temporary. When the quilt top is complete, you will turn it back to its original position.

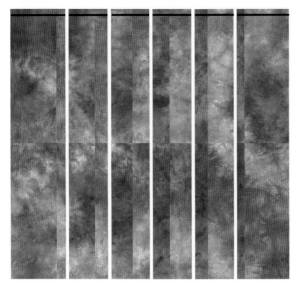

Sew strips in pairs.

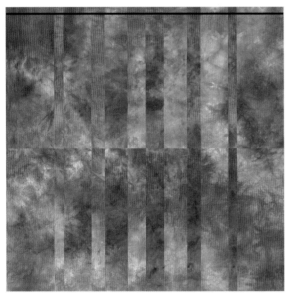

The first half of the Harmonic Convergence is complete.

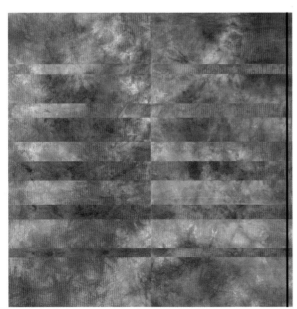

Reposition the quilt so the strips are horizontal.

TIP 1 There are 12 strips. Position Strips 1 and 2 right sides together and sew from top to bottom. Note that Strip 2 is narrow and is positioned on top of Strip 1, which is wider. Sew the next pair, Strips 3 and 4, top to bottom. Again, the narrower strip is on top. As you move from one pair to the next, notice that the strip on top gets wider while the strip underneath gets narrower. The final pair of strips will have a wide strip positioned on top of a narrow strip. After you sew each seam, place the pair back into the "puzzle" and make sure that all the strips are positioned correctly.

TIP 2 Match the seams as best you can. You can use a pin if you prefer. If you don't get them to match perfectly, leave them alone. This seam will soon be cut out and tossed away. Also, if you get to the end of a seam on the outside edge of the quilt and it doesn't match perfectly, don't worry about it. The ends can be trimmed off later when you square the top in preparation for borders.

12. Mark a new orientation line ¼" or less from the top edge of the quilt.

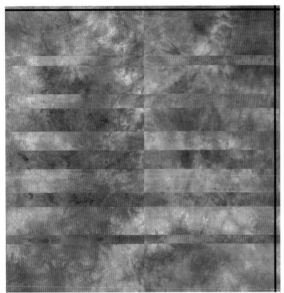

Add a new reference line.

13. Remove the center seam by trimming approximately ¼" on each side of the vertical seam. When you are preparing to cut out the vertical seam, you may find that it is slightly tilted. If this happens, it is more important for the cut to be perpendicular to the horizontal seams than for the cut to be parallel with the vertical seam.

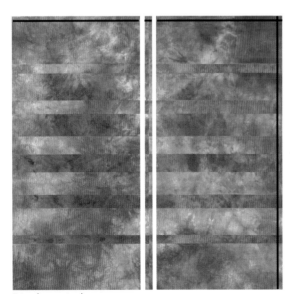

Trim the vertical seam.

14. Before you go any further, take one of the halves (it doesn't matter which one) and press the seams in the opposite direction. Once the next set of strips is cut, the seams will alternate without having to re-press each strip individually.

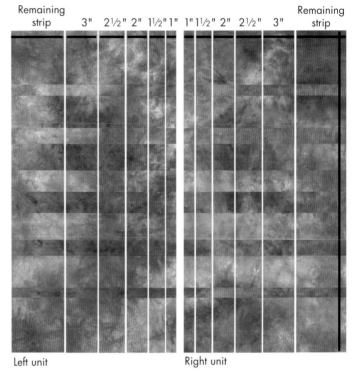

Cut strips as indicated.

15. The process begins just as before. The left unit is cut with a right edge gradation, and the right unit is cut using a left edge gradation. Refer to the Strip Measurement Chart on page 29 to cut the strips.

16. As before, move Strip 1 (the 1" strip) of the left unit between Strips 5 and 6 of the right unit.

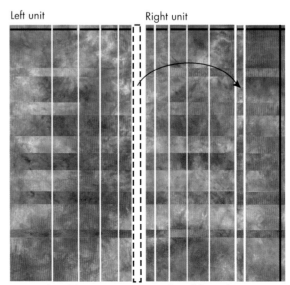

Strip 1 placed between Strips 5 and 6 of the right unit.

17. Move Strip 2 (the 1½" strip) from the left unit between Strips 4 and 5 of the right unit.

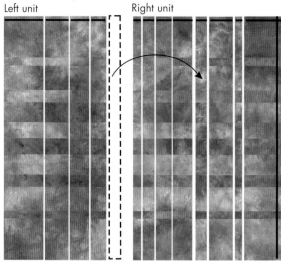

Left unit   Right unit

Move the next strip.

18. Continue positioning strips from the left unit between strips of the right unit until all the strips are converged. As before, the strips from the right unit automatically end up in their correct positions. Sew the strips from left to right or, if you prefer, in pairs as before. If you have cut, sewn, and pressed accurately, you will have no trouble matching the seams as you sew.

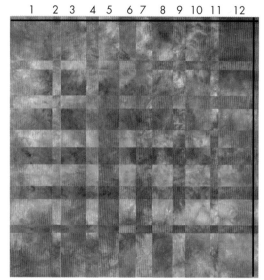

The strips are converged and sewn together.

A completed Original Harmonic Convergence quilt top

19. Turn the quilt back to its original position with the first orientation line at the top. Square the quilt by trimming the outside edges.

The magic is not over. Choices for borders will greatly affect the outcome of the overall design. Study the quilts in the galleries to see examples of creative borders. Borders are discussed on page 73.

Gallery: Harmonic Convergence Quilts

The quilts in this gallery are all Harmonic Convergence quilts with pieced borders. It is amazing to see the creativity and diversity in these quilts. Often a simplistic border creates a gentle elegance, while complex borders evoke imaginative and wild expressions. Look closely and learn how the fabrics relate to one another. Note that many of these quilts have a window of light represented by one particular fabric. Use the knowledge you gain by studying these quilts when you make your own Harmonic Convergence quilt.

Behind the Waterfall by Carolyn Sherman, Colorado Springs, Colorado, 33" x 34", 2002

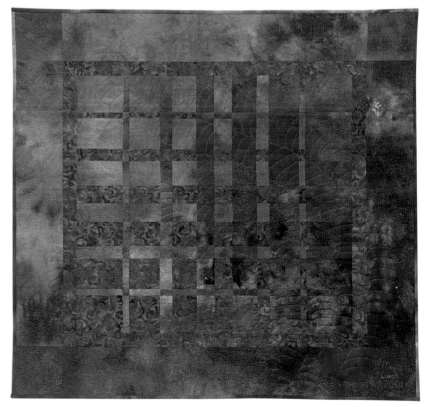

Flying with Ricky by Meg Leach, Andover, England, 32" x 30", 2001

Jubilee by Patricia C. Kilmark, Atlanta, Georgia, 31'' x 30'', 2002

Reflections on Loch Lomond by Maureen Anderson, Helensburgh, Scotland, 33'' x 32'', 2001

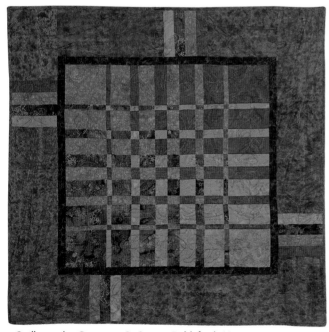

Guillaume by Georgette R. Sutton, Biddeford, Maine, 42'' x 41'', 2002

A Fabric Monet by Donna E. Johnson, Naples, Florida, 34'' x 34'', 2000

Colors of the Desert
by Ellen P. Brooks,
Lancaster, California,
27" x 29", 2002

*Convergence
of Leaves* by
Barbara
Sandberg,
Victoria, Texas,
32" x 33",
2002

*Harmonic
Convergence*
by Dani Fisk,
Wrightwood,
California,
29" x 30",
2001

*Blue-Green
Convergence* by
Lynn Koolish,
Berkeley,
California,
36" x 36", 2001

Zebras Converging
by Carole Johnson,
Zebulon, North
Carolina,
35" x 33", 2002

Nightfall by Diane Powers Harris, Miami, Florida, 38" x 43", 2002

My Wings are Back by Helen Deighan, Grayshott, Surrey, England, 29" x 31", 2001

Floral Medley by Alice E. Hill, Fountain Hills, Arizona, 30" x 30", 2002

Forest Fugue by Leslie Rovainen, Brookings, Oregon, 33" x 32", 2000

Gallery: Gloriously Appliquéd Convergence Quilts

In class, I will often have someone who is less than pleased with his/her Harmonic Convergence quilt. In most cases, the student has a limited understanding of the many variations because they have only seen *my* quilts, which feature my hand-dyed fabric. Naturally, this presents a lopsided perspective of how one of these quilts should look. I don't want students making quilts that look just like mine, nor do I want to make quilts that look like theirs. The beauty of self-expression comes in the uniqueness of the individual. When I encounter a student whose quilt just isn't to their liking, I encourage them to keep going by adding borders and perhaps appliqué to enhance the effect.

In this gallery, the artists used a basic Harmonic Convergence quilt as the background for appliqué. In some cases, the original quilt became almost secondary to the details that were added. By exploring the possibilities of appliqué, the artists made the quilts come to life. The Harmonic Convergence became a backdrop for the drama of creativity.

Spring Blooms by Gloria Korn, Yardley, Pennsylvania, 24" x 22", 2002

Mother's Day in the Japanese Tea Garden by Linda Easley, Sanger, California, 29" x 30", 2002

Into the Light by Lee Paget, Woking, England, 32" x 32", 2001

Lombok Sunset by Diane Romero Mattern, Tehachapi,
California, 38" x 38", 2002

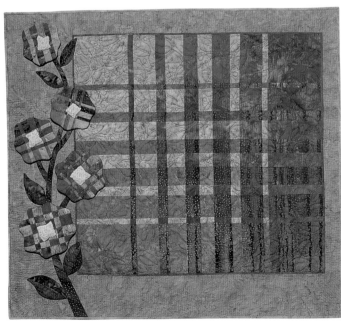

Dream Garden Quilt by Donna Kohler, Fresno, California,
38" x 34", 2002

Harmonic Convergence Goes Hawaiian by Joan Waldman,
Platte Center, Nebraska, 32" x 32", 2002

Rage by Andrea Perejda, Arroyo Grande, California, 25'' x 26'', 2000

Sultry Susans by Terry Waldron, Anaheim, California,
32'' x 32'', 2001

Petals on the Path by Gloria Korn, Yardley, Pennsylvania,
24'' x 23'', 2002

Tropical Paradise by Sharon Dreger, Kaukauna, Wisconsin, 28'' x 29'', 2002

RT's Remember December by Ione Ewert Whitney,
Port Orchard, Washington, 30" x 31", 2001

Autumn Glow by Jeanne L. Pfister, Kaukauna, Wisconsin, 30" x 29", 2002

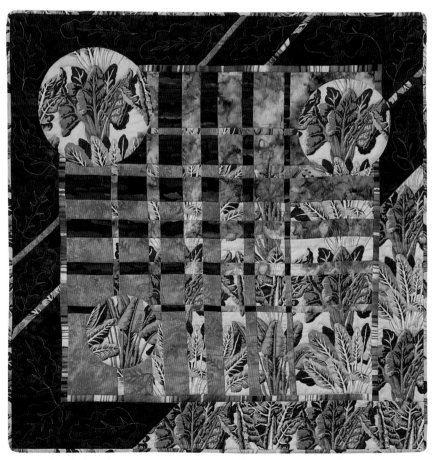

Great Balls of Chard by Lorri Brown Wolfe, quilted by Judy Hooper, Colfax, California,
34" x 35", 2003

Divide and Conquer Convergence

The Divide and Conquer Convergence is an easy variation that teaches you how to cut and sew curves without using templates or fussing over perfect ¼" seams. This improvisational and unorthodox approach is amazingly easy and will undoubtedly inspire you to experiment on your own. For this project, layer two fabrics and cut them with gentle curves. Rearrange the resulting pieces and sew them together to create two new blocks. Cut the blocks into strips and converge. Please try not to plan too much; it is more enjoyable and rewarding to let the design unfold with each step.

Basic Supplies

You will need two fabrics (fat quarters are perfect; the squares used are about 16" square), a sharp rotary cutter and large mat, fabric markers and, of course, your sewing machine.

Fabric Selection

This variation starts with just two fabrics. I usually cut both of my starting squares slightly larger than I need from a single piece of multi-colored, hand-dyed fabric. However, there are many commercial fabrics that are appropriate. Try to use two contrasting fabrics that have an overall color or print. Experiment with a multicolored fabric and a commercial batik. I warn against using two large-scale prints or two fabrics that have a similar appearance. Try to select fabrics that will allow the pieced curves to be the dominant element in the design.

Remember, don't fuss too much over fabric choices. I've learned the best approach is to try it and see. There are several Divide and Conquer Convergence quilts on pages 49–52. You will notice that they utilize a variety of fabrics. Although some of these might have initially lacked interest or pizazz, the creative extras added by the artist, such as appliqué, unique borders, and decorative quilting, helped change an ordinary project into an extraordinary quilt.

Steps for a Divide and Conquer Convergence

1. Layer two pressed, unstarched fabrics *right sides up* on a cutting mat. Without using a ruler, freely cut a square with your rotary cutter. The square should be approximately 16" on each side, give or take an inch or so. I know you will be tempted to grab the ruler to cut your squares, but you don't have to. The two contrasting fabrics only need to be *sorta* square and *sorta* 16". Because you cut the two fabrics at the same time, both right sides up, they will be identical in shape and size—*sorta*.

When cutting without a ruler, you may create ripples in your fabrics as you cut. To avoid this, hold the fabric at the edge and gently tug while cutting. This is the safest hand position.

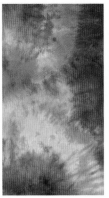 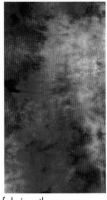

Choose two contrasting fabrics; these are
from the same piece.

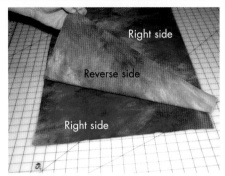

Right side

Reverse side

Right side

Layer them both *right sides up.*

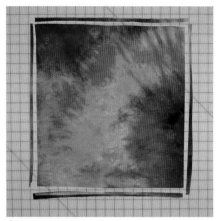

Cut an approximate 16" square.

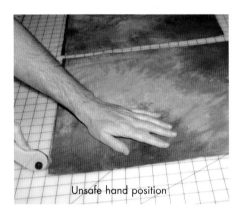

Unsafe hand position

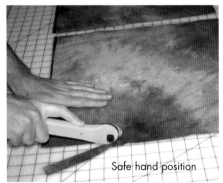

Safe hand position

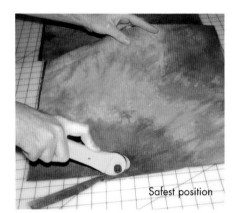

Safest position

Hold the edge.

2. With your layered squares still positioned right sides up on the mat,
cut 2 *gentle* undulating curves that flow diagonally across the square.
I like to create a tornado-like shape that is wide on one side and
narrow on the other. You might find it helpful to draw the curves first
with a fabric marker or pencil. If cutting fabric without a ruler is new
to you, you might feel unsure and timid. You will gain confidence as
you gain experience.

SAFETY TIPS: When cutting without a ruler,
never place your non-cutting hand as if
you were using a ruler. Always place it
away from, or behind, the blade. Notice
the three examples above.

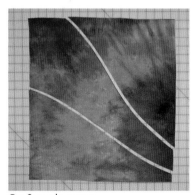

Cut 2 gentle curves.

3. Separate the blocks so they are side by side with the
pieces in their original positions. If you are using
fabrics that don't have a distinct right side, be sure to
take extra care not to turn one of the pieces upside
down when separating the blocks.

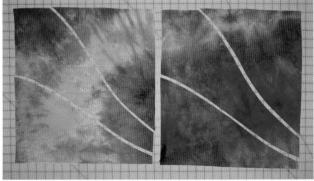

Position the blocks side by side.

4. Exchange the middle pieces in each block, but don't sew them together just yet.

Middle pieces swapped.

5. Before sewing, play with the orientation of the two blocks. The goal is to cut each block into vertical strips and converge them into each other. Each block has the potential to be turned a quarter turn in any direction, providing several possible convergence options. I like to orient the two blocks differently. Here are a few placement options.

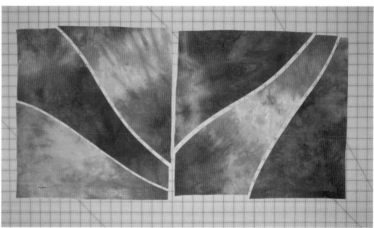

One of the ways to orient the blocks before converging

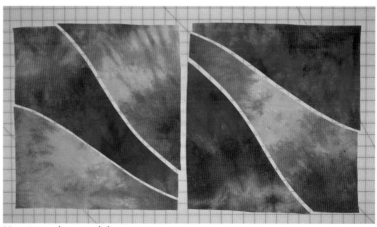

Here is another possibility.

6. If you have reversible fabrics—fabrics with no obvious right and wrong sides—you also have the option of turning one or both blocks upside down, creating even more options for orienting your blocks.

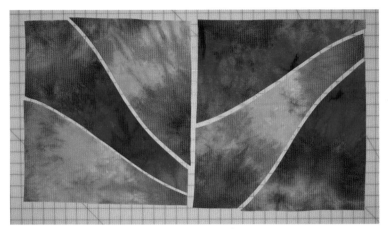

The right block is turned to the wrong/reverse side.

7. Once you choose the orientation of your blocks, use a distinct fabric marker to make registration marks about every 2" across the curves, as shown. When you gain confidence sewing these free-form curves, you may want to stop making registration marks. I don't usually make registration marks for seams shorter than 18", but I do recommend making them for larger, longer curves, or if improvisational patchwork is new to you. The following example shows the registration marks.

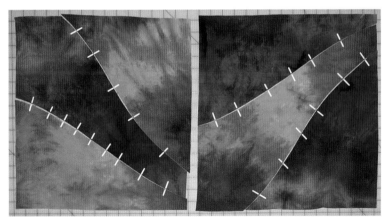

Draw registration marks.

I'm often asked if it matters which curve is on top—the convex or the concave. In some traditional patchwork blocks it matters, but because these seams follow a gentle "S" curve, the convex curve will change to the concave curve as the seam is sewn. Therefore, it doesn't matter. I am more likely to put the "new" piece (the piece that is being added to the patchwork) on top, regardless of the curve.

8. Position the first two pieces right sides together. Notice that the curves go in opposite directions.

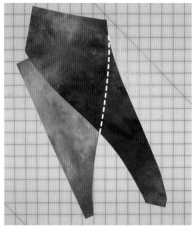

Curves go in opposite directions.

9. Bring the edges into position as you sew, easing or tugging to match the registration marks. The curves are gentle, and there is no need to pin them. Sew the pieces together using a narrow seam allowance, smaller than 1/4". Because no seam allowance was included on the piece, it is important to sew the smallest secure seam possible. As you sew the seam, make sure you can see a hairline of the bottom fabric to ensure that you are sewing both fabrics together. You may also find that the ends don't match when the seam is completed. This is normal and should be expected.

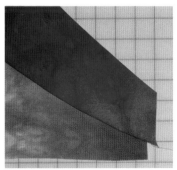

A completed seam

A mist bottle or steam can convince a block to lie flat.

10. To press the seam, I prefer to mist the unit with water, but steaming works equally well. Unlike traditional patchwork, you will need the moisture to persuade the block to lie flat. Position the block right side up, and hold the newly sewn piece up. Press into the seam, forcing the seam allowance only one direction, and create a tight, crisp seam. Repeat for each seam.

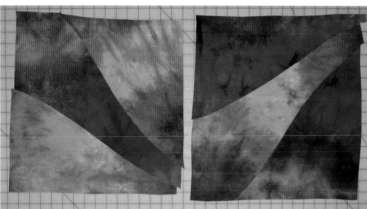

Two untrimmed, completed blocks

11. Complete both blocks by sewing and pressing in the manner described above.

Press from the center out.

12. As you complete each block, lay it right side up and press. Begin in the center and slowly and firmly press out to the edges, in the direction of the bias. Gently tug the bias as you press, if this helps to flatten the block. Allow the moisture to relax the fibers, and press firmly to flatten the block. Remember it is all right if the edges of the block become distorted. It is more important that the block is flat.

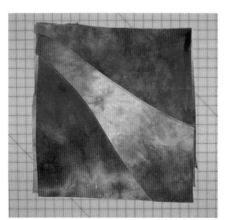

Blocks with right sides together

13. Reposition both blocks right sides up, side by side, in the same position you had previously determined. Imagine that the two blocks are an open book. Close the book by folding the right block over onto the left block. Now imagine that you are looking at the back of the book and the spine is along the right edge. The blocks are now positioned right sides together.

14. Use a ruler to straighten the right and top edges of the two blocks. There is no need to trim the left or bottom at this point.

Straighten the top and right edges.

15. Cut both blocks simultaneously with a right edge gradation. Beginning on the newly trimmed right edge, cut a 1" strip. Each subsequent strip will be ½" larger than the previous strip. Stop cutting strips when it becomes obvious that the last strip will be narrower than the previous strip. I prefer the final strip to be the widest strip. Leave the outside edge ragged. It will be trimmed later.

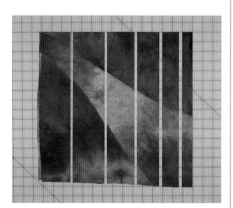
Cut using a right edge gradation.

16. The top (wrong-side up) block needs to be turned back to its original position, one strip at a time. Begin with the narrowest strip, and place it right side up in its original position next to the left block. Remove the next strip of the top block, and position it right side up next to the previous strip. Continue putting each strip back into its original position. If you position the strips correctly, the two blocks will be in their original orientation with no strips jumbled or inverted.

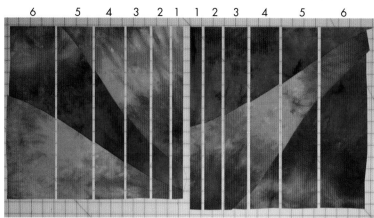
The blocks are in their original positions.

17. Converge the strips. Take the 1" strip (Strip 1) of the left unit and insert it between Strips 5 and 6 of the right unit. This is the same method described in Steps 5–7 on pages 29–30. The right unit has to shuffle to the left each time a strip from the left unit is inserted. You may find it helpful to know that you only have to pick up and move strips from the left block. As the right block shuffles left and separates to make room for the inserted strips, the strips of the right block automatically end up where they belong.

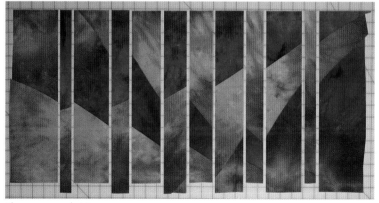
The converged strips

You may wonder if you should sew the strips alternately: top to bottom, then bottom to top. You can, and should, if you find that your seams tend to bend once they are sewn and pressed. If you find it necessary to sew the strips alternately, then trim the bottom edges of all the strips before sewing, so you can match the bottom edges of the strips when you sew.

You may ask, "Should I sew the strips in pairs?" For longer strips and seams, I often sew in pairs from top to bottom. Then I sew the pairs together from bottom to top. However, for the short seams in this project, I find that it is unnecessary to sew alternately or in pairs.

18. Sew the strips together from top to bottom. The top edge was trimmed previously, so the top edges of the strips would match. The bottom edges do not need to match at this point. I recommend that you dry-press each seam once it is completed. Although the curved seams were distorted and forced flat by misting or steam, these straight seams should remain straight and undistorted. Use a dry iron and press the seams in one direction.

Strips are sewn and the top is ready for trimming.

19. Give the completed Divide and Conquer Convergence a final press and square it up as desired. Add borders and quilt.

The completed quilt top

Gallery: Divide and Conquer Convergence Quilts

Divide and Conquer Convergence quilts are a lot of fun to make, but sometimes the results can be hit or miss. The fabric choices make a huge difference in the way the quilt looks once the strips are converged. One important thing to remember is that these quilts are so fast to make you will have only spent a few minutes and used a small amount of fabric.

Let's not downplay the excitement of Divide and Conquer Convergence quilts; the quilts in this gallery are amazing. Divide and Conquer was the base for all of these quilts. I can attest to the fact that some of these quilts were rather blah before the quiltmaker's creativity took over. It was a good challenge, because it allowed the artist to use the design to create a quilt with exciting undulations and movement, treating the viewer to a spectacular visual journey.

I R Happy by Bridget Wilson Matlock, Alcoa, Tennessee, 31" x 38", 2001

Just for Fun by Shirlee Boarts, Ford City, Pennsylvania, 24'' x 23'', 2002

Ghost Spirit Road I by Christi Bonds, Reno, Nevada, 33'' x 24'', 2002

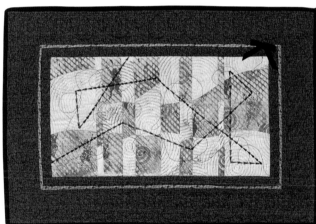

Joyce Met Ricky in Baton Rouge by Elvia Edwards, Poplarville, Mississippi, 24'' x 16'', 2001

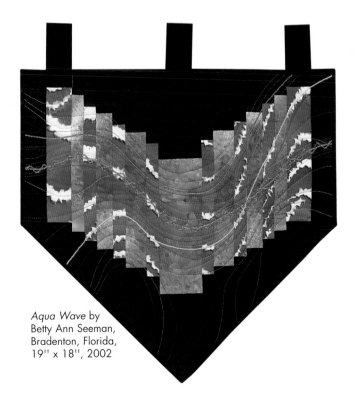

Aqua Wave by Betty Ann Seeman, Bradenton, Florida, 19'' x 18'', 2002

Sunrise by Claire Waquespack Fenton, Houma, Louisiana,
48'' x 38'', 2001

Sea of Qi I by Christi Bonds, Reno, Nevada, 40" x 37", 2002

Baby's Harmonic Convergence by Becky S. Poisson, Boulder Creek,
California, 31'' x 36'', 2002

Deep Blue Harmonies by Lori Cammie Rice, Cary, North Carolina,
36'' x 27'', 2002

Jungle Cat Convergence
by Laura Cotter, Tucson,
Arizona, 22" x 17", 2002

Blowin' in the Wind
by Betty Ann Seeman,
Bradenton, Florida,
21" x 11", 2002

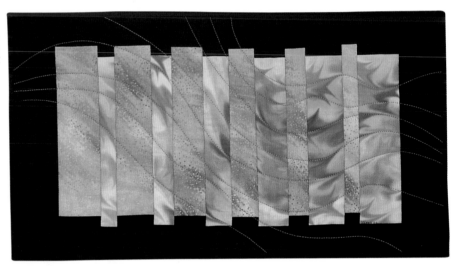

Bio Tech by Lorri Brown Wolfe,
quilted by Judy Hooper, Colfax,
California, 36" x 39", 2003

Grand Convergence

So the original Harmonic Convergence and the Divide and Conquer Convergence were a piece of cake. Hungry for more, for something a bit grander? You will love making a Grand Convergence, I promise.

To begin a Grand Convergence quilt, you create a patchwork panel with several flowing curves. The panel is then sliced into strips and converged with strips from another fabric. Another possibility is to use two pieced panels, and cut both into strips that are then converged together.

The project is generally larger than the Divide and Conquer Convergence, so there will be some significant differences in the way the patchwork is constructed. As you have learned, you create the Divide and Conquer Convergence by cutting two layers of fabric at once. The Grand Convergence differs in that you make templates for each piece in the design, and then cut the individual pieces from several fabrics. Because the design has longer curved seams, registration marks are necessary to ensure flat patchwork and good workmanship.

Here are several designs that work well for this project.

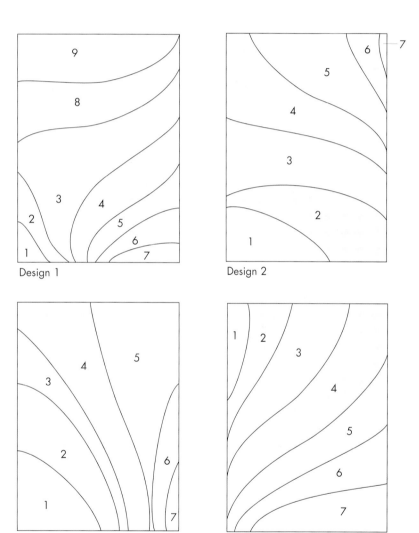

Design 1

Design 2

Design 3

Design 4

Notice that the designs have a strong diagonal/horizontal flow. I prefer to create convergences with vertical strips. I choose a design with diagonal/horizontal flow, so it will remain prominent and effective in the final quilt. If I created a convergence with horizontal strips, I would choose a design with a diagonal/vertical flow, so the design would be obvious after the convergence.

A Word About Proportions

Notice that the designs are not confined within a square shape. Instead, they are created in vertical rectangles. I've learned that the final width of a vertical convergence will increase (perhaps even double) as vertical strips are inserted. It won't get taller, but it will get wider. Therefore, if I start with a tall, vertical rectangular design, the overall height/width ratio is not so extreme once vertical strips are converged.

Conversely, if I want to create a horizontal convergence, I will probably start with a wide, rectangular horizontal design. The design will gain height when horizontal strips are inserted. If I start with a design that is wider than it is tall, it won't seem so out of proportion when horizontal strips are converged. The horizontal rectangle (landscape orientation) is likely to expand and become a vertical rectangle (portrait orientation) once the strips are converged.

Basic Supplies

For this project, you will need to gather several fabrics, a sharp rotary cutter, a very large mat, freezer paper, fabric markers, and your sewing machine.

Steps for a Grand Convergence

1. Tape pieces of freezer paper together along the factory-cut edge. A good starting size for this project is 24" wide x 36" tall, but you can make it any size you wish.

2. Create a design on the freezer paper with several swoops. Use any of the designs provided above, or create your own.

The one used here is similar, but not identical, to Design 1. Try drawing the designs freehand. If you don't feel confident drawing freehand, you can make a transparent copy of one of the designs on page 53, and enlarge it using an overhead projector.

3. Number the piecing order, and mark lines to indicate the straight grain. Using a colored marker, make registration marks 1"–2" apart along each drawn line.

Design with numbered pieces and registration marks

4. Cut the templates and pin them in order on a design wall.

Templates on a design wall

Freezer paper is on a roll, so it tends to curl. Iron the dull side of the paper for a few seconds. The shiny side will stick to your ironing surface, but when you pull it off, it will be flatter and easier to handle. If you iron quickly, with a light hand, the freezer paper will retain its stickiness to use with your selected fabric.

5. Choose fabrics for the different templates. Some of the swoops seem like flowing ribbons, while others work better as background pieces. Decide what fabric you want for each template. Iron the first template shiny side down to the right side of your first fabric.

Iron template to the right side of the fabric.

6. Using the edge of the template as a guide, cut the fabric, leaving only a slight seam allowance.

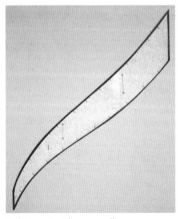

Fabric cut with seam allowance

7. Transfer the registration marks from the paper to the fabric. Use a marker that will contrast with the fabric and make the registration marks easy to see when you are sewing.

Transfer the registration marks onto the seam allowance.

8. Remove the paper and place the fabric piece into position on the design wall.

Fabric piece on the design wall

9. Repeat Steps 5–8 with each of the other templates.

10. Sew the pieces together in order with a narrow seam allowance, matching registration marks as you sew. The curves are gentle, so there is no need to pin. You may pin if you prefer, but it is usually not necessary on these gentle curves. Always make sure you can see a hairline of the bottom fabric as you sew.

Press each seam after it is sewn. Don't worry if the edges are crooked; they are straightened as you cut strips.

Pieces in position and ready for sewing

11. Now it's time to cut strips and converge them with another fabric. As you have learned, the possibilities are endless. See the two options on pages 56 and 57.

Pieces sewn together

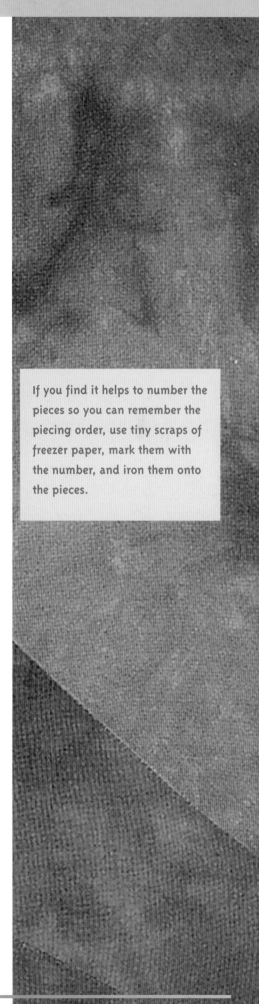

If you find it helps to number the pieces so you can remember the piecing order, use tiny scraps of freezer paper, mark them with the number, and iron them onto the pieces.

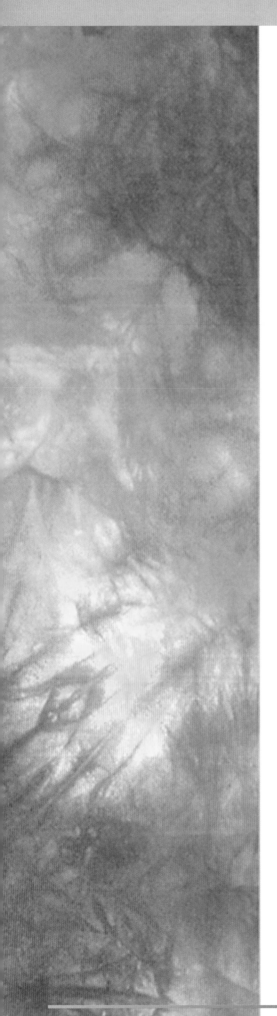

OPTION A

1. Cut the pieced unit into same-size strips; 2" is a reasonable width, but you can choose other sizes as well.

2. Converge the strips with another fabric that is cut with an inside-out gradation (see page 17). Remember, if you have an even number of 2" strips from the pieced unit, you will need an odd number of strips from the convergence fabric.

3. Cut the pieced unit into 10 strips, and the convergence fabric into 11 strips.

This example shows a single, narrow strip in the middle. The convergence strips get wider as they move outward.

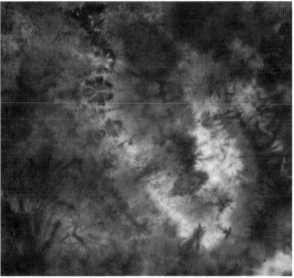

Convergence fabric

Option A: 2" strips from the pieced converged unit with an inside-out gradation with one narrow center strip

OPTION B

1. Cut the pieced unit into same-size strips, 2" perhaps.
2. Converge these strips with spacer strips (also 2") from a separate fabric.

If the pieced unit creates an even number of 2" strips, then you will need an odd number of 2" strips of the convergence fabric.

Don't forget that borders can greatly enhance a design. Below is an example of Option B with borders added.

I encourage you to create your own designs for a Grand Convergence. The quilt can be any size. Just remember that the design will expand when converged, so plan your estimated final proportions accordingly.

Option B: all same-size strips

Option B with borders

Blended Convergence

By now I hope your mind is spinning with your own convergence possibilities. Before you begin exploring your own "what ifs," try one final Convergence variation. This is perhaps the easiest of them all, and the results are spectacular. Get ready for the magical Blended Convergence.

In this method, all the strips are cut in even widths. The main difference between a Blended Convergence and all other Convergence quilts is that the strips are not sorted into a new order before they are sewn together. Only a true quilter would find a reason to cut fabric into strips and then immediately sew it back together, right? Nonetheless, that is how the Blended Convergence works.

Basic Supplies

For this project, you will need just one yard of a rather spectacular fabric, a sharp rotary cutter, a very large mat, and your sewing machine.

Fabric Selection

The fabric you select for this project makes a big difference in the success of the final quilt. Multicolored hand-dyed fabrics are perfect. If you come across a fabric with a very large print, it also might create an interesting illusion.

Steps for a Blended Convergence

1. Cut the fabric into strips. In most cases, I prefer to cut 2"-wide strips, although other widths are certainly possible. Begin your first Blended Convergence project by cutting 2" strips; you can experiment with other widths later.

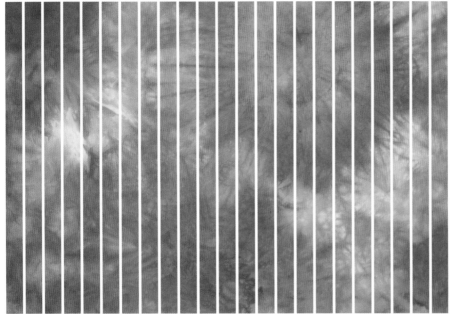

One yard cut into 2" strips

2. Do not rearrange the strips. Sew the strips back together with an accurate and consistent seam allowance. I recommend shifting the strips up and down 1" or so, as indicated in the illustration. Doing so will enable you to see the design's transformation. Press the strips in one direction.

Offset strips sewn together

3. Turn the quilt so the strips are now horizontal, and cut 2" strips.

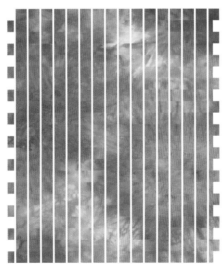

Turn and cut into 2" strips.

4. Re-press the seam allowance of every other strip in the opposite direction. Sew the strips together, shifting the squares alternately across the top as indicated. Carefully match each seam as you sew. Every other strip should be shifted one square from its original position.

Offset strips sewn together a second time

5. Trim the top, bottom, and sides as desired.
6. Add borders. This easy, magical, and quick quilt is complete!

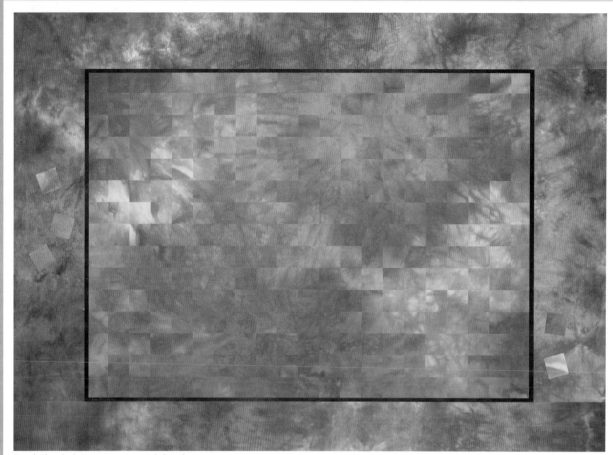

Final Blended Convergence with borders

Hey folks, it doesn't get any easier that that! You may have already noticed that the Blended Convergence is a perfect background for appliqué and decorative quilting. I love seeing what happens to these fabrics when I use this method.

There are other variations that create incredible possibilities. Allow me to show you one very simple Blended Convergence variation.

Blended Convergence Variation

1. Begin with two fabrics: Fabric A is 22" wide, Fabric B is 20" wide. Both are 36" tall. Place side by side as indicated.
2. Slice both fabrics into 2"-wide strips. Fabric A will yield 11 strips and Fabric B will yield 10 strips.

Remember that no strips were rearranged, sorted, or converged in the basic Blended Convergence instructions. In this variation, you converge the two sets of strips.

Fabric A   Fabric B

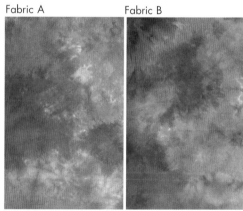

Two fabrics side by side

Fabric A, 11 strips   Fabric B, 10 strips

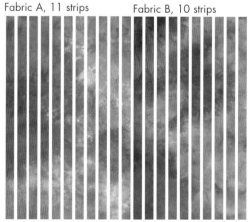

Cut 2" strips from each fabric.

3. Separate the 11 strips from Fabric A to make room for the 10 strips from Fabric B. Converge the two together. After the strips are converged, sew them together. There is no need to shift the strips. Simply match the tops and sew them, in order or in pairs, as you prefer. Press the seams in one direction.

Sew strips together.

4. Turn the quilt top a quarter turn so the strips are horizontal.

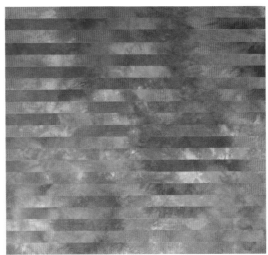

Turn the quilt top.

5. Cut the quilt top into as many 2" strips as you can.

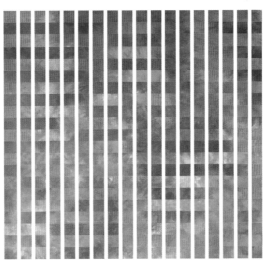

Cut into 2" strips.

6. Re-press the seams of every other strip in the opposite direction. As before, shift every other strip by one square as you sew the strips together. Carefully match the seams as you sew.

7. Once the top is completed, trim the edges as desired.

8. Add borders, then quilt.

By now, you are most likely pondering the endless possibilities of Convergence quilts. As you have already learned, none of these quilts takes a tremendous amount of time, and they are easy! As wall quilts or garments, dorm room decorations or backgrounds for appliqué, these quilts can serve a multitude of purposes, and they are a delight to all who make them, as well as to all who receive them.

Shift the rows, then sew the strips together.

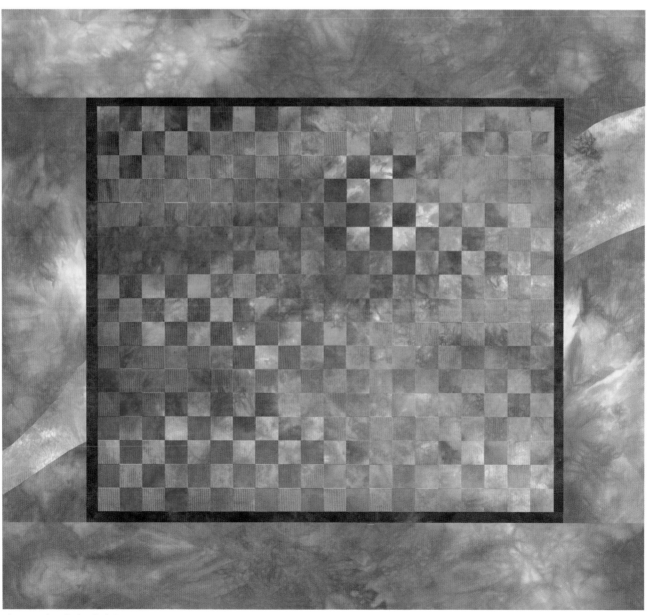

The completed Blended Convergence variation

Virtual Incentives

The world of digital technology has certainly changed the way most of us live. It is no different in the world of quilting. Here are three virtual quilts that will help you better understand the distribution of fabrics in a Harmonic Convergence quilt. These samples give you the opportunity to watch a Convergence quilt come together. Enjoy the magic as it unfolds in the following illustrations.

Harmonic Convergence: *Golden Harvest*

This convergence demonstrates how four rather ordinary commercial prints can make an outstanding Harmonic Convergence quilt.

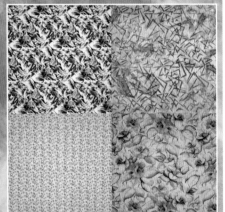

Start with four fabrics.

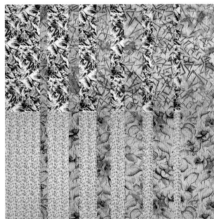

Vertical convergence

Horizontal convergence

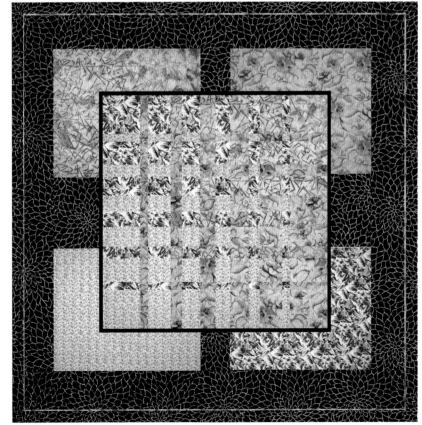

What a difference borders can make!

Harmonic Convergence: *Blue Lagoon*

For this quilt, I selected two hand-dyed fabrics and two commercial fabrics. Notice that the large-print fish fabric stands alone. It remains prominent in the final quilt.

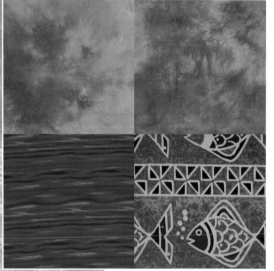
Start with four coordinating fabrics.

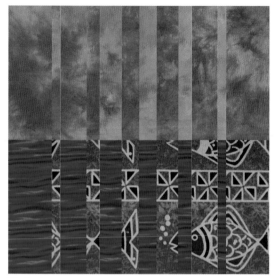
Vertical convergence

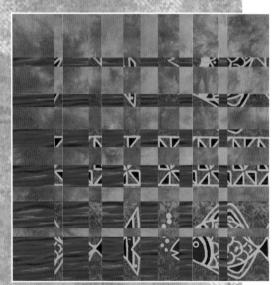
Horizontal convergence

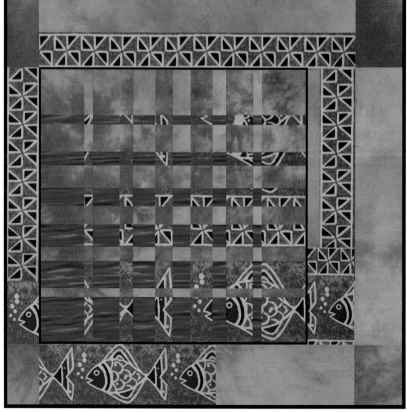
Use borders to express your creativity.

Harmonic Convergence: *Serendipity*

The commercial prints in *Serendipity* are diverse. I chose the red fabric because I knew it would break up the overall design. The large-scale print has a diagonal flow that works well in the overall design.

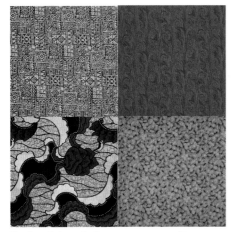

The four fabrics before convergence. The focus fabric (the large print) is in the bottom-left corner.

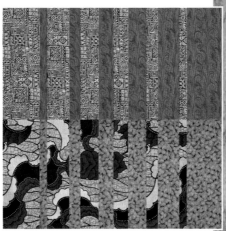

Vertical convergence

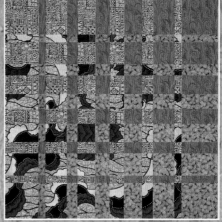

Full vertical and horizontal convergence

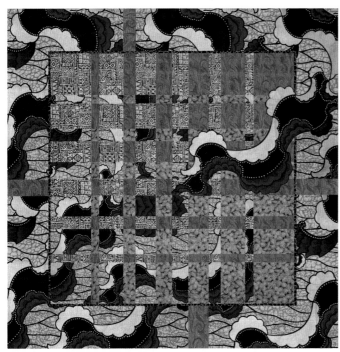

I used the focus fabric in the border with simple strips of red. A *Broderie Perse* appliqué from the large print is added to the quilt top.

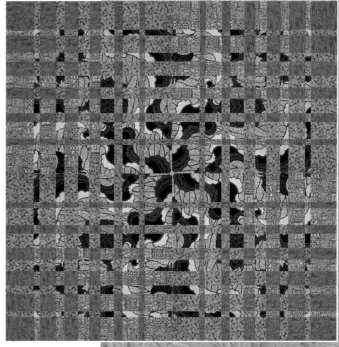

Here is a great "what if" Four identical Harmonic Convergence quilts joined with the focal fabric facing the center.

Gallery: Explorations of "What If"

All of the artists represented in this gallery have one thing in common. Regarding the principles of Convergence quilts, they already know the sky is the limit. When I look at these quilts, I can actually see their minds spinning with ideas. I know that the "what if" question gnawed at them as they sipped a cup of coffee, drove the kids to school, or tended a flowerbed. I'm sure more than a few idle moments were stolen at work because the "what if" question crept up on them like a curious creative cat. They couldn't rest until they found the answer. Take a look at the amazing quilts that have resulted from such a distracting little question: What if?

Spastic Inspirations by Mary L. Penton, Huntsville, Alabama, 52" x 66", 2002

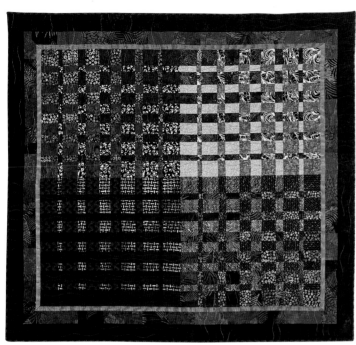

What If by Joan Sievenpiper, quilted by Robin Saunders, St. Charles, Illinois, 45'' x 45'', 2002

HC x 4 by Judith Putnam, Paris, Tennessee, 52'' x 48'', 2002

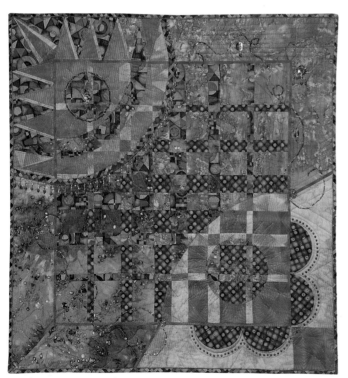

Illusions Galore by Lorri Brown Wolfe, quilted by Judy Hooper, Colfax, California, 43'' x 46'', 2003

Sunshine Convergence by Nancy Kay Smith, Miami, Florida, 31'' x 33'', 2002

Ricky Tims and Katie
went to the seashore, the winds were blowing, the waves
were cresting, the sun was shining all together in one
glorious harmonic convergence....

Ricky Tims and Katie at the Seashore by Kathleen "Katie" Ehrhardt,
Los Angeles, California, 40" x 48", 2002

Paradise Beckons by Cathy Pope, Littleton, Colorado, 43" x 43", 2002

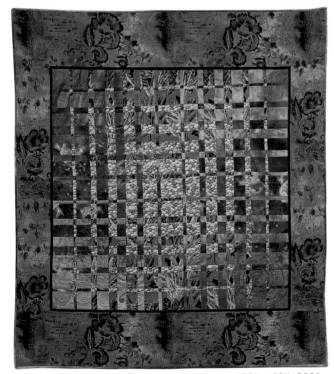

Chard Dye-It by JoAnn Belling, Des Moines, Iowa, 52" x 58", 2001

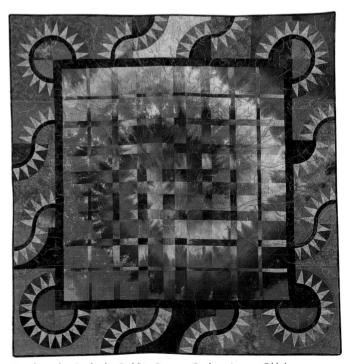

Breaking the Cycles by Debbie Denton, Broken Arrow, Oklahoma,
54" x 54", 2001

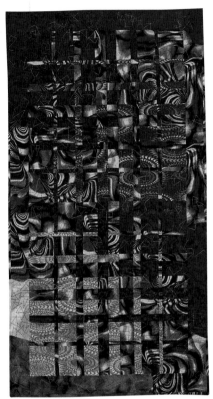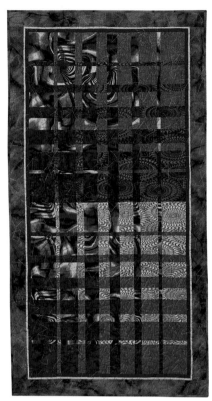

Only in My Dreams (left) and Growing Up Strong (right) by Sandy Baglio, Apex, North Carolina, both 27'' x 51'', 2002

Food Hole I by Christi Bonds, Reno, Nevada, 57'' x 58'', 2002

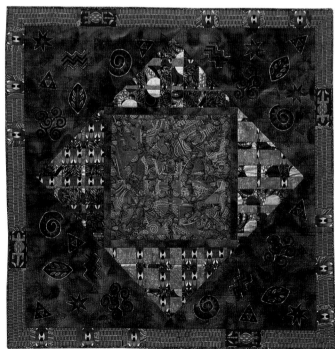

Amistad by Liana E. Miller, as a Round Robin quilt made with Diana Harris, Louise Regan, and Mary DeWind, Miami, Florida, 41''x 41'', 2002

Harmonic Diversity: A Prayer for 9/11 by Cindy Neville, St. Louis, Missouri, 38" x 38", 2002

Mighty Rivers by Art Kruse, Kirkwood, Missouri, man's vest, 2002

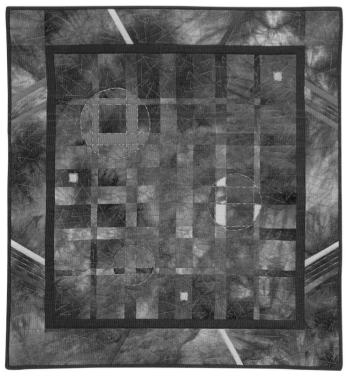

Circles of Life Emerging from the Universe by Marleen Gustafson, Menomonee Falls, Wisconsin, 29" x 31", 2002

Raccoon Reggae by Diane Powers Harris, Miami, Florida, woman's vest, 2002

Harmonic Convergence Table Runner by Brenda Carlson, Lincoln, Nebraska, 16" x 46", 2000

Transitions by Devi Town, Colorado Springs, Colorado, 25" x 21", 1999

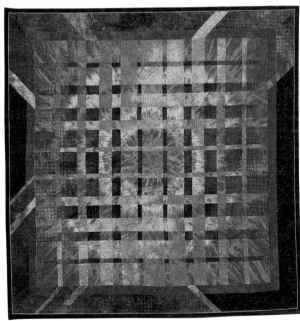

Sunrise by Cindy Vough, Nicholasville, Kentucky, 33" x 33", 2002

Quilt Puzzle I: Indian Summer by Ann Gail Peterson, Davis, California, 41" x 41", 2002

Loose Ends

Troubleshooting a Convergence

SQUARING A DESIGN

I prefer to wait until the convergence is complete before I square the quilt. Some of my students had problems squaring their Harmonic Convergence quilt until they realized the height and width measurements were different. Well, first of all, let me remind you that once the vertical strips are converged, an approximate 1/2" slice is taken from the center and tossed aside. That forces the top to be slightly rectangular instead of square. If you want it to be square, trim the excess off of the outside and square it before adding frames or borders.

If you have used starch, cut carefully, used consistent seam allowances, and pressed accurately, the interior of the quilt will be square. If it has a tendency to be slightly off, block it on an ironing mat using the smallest, outermost seam as your reference. See page 74 for blocking tips.

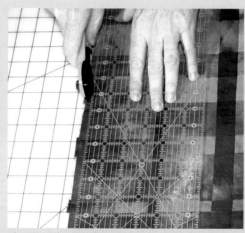

The 3 1/2" line on the ruler is aligned with the outermost seam of the quilt.

Do not attempt to use the outside edges of the quilt as a reference for measuring and trimming. The outside edge will be trimmed according to the outermost sewn seam.

MY SEAMS DON'T MATCH!

As I mentioned before, I'm not the quilt police, and I'm not going to fault you for a seam that doesn't match. However, if you are interested in getting the seams to match, remember there are three steps to accurate piecing: cutting, sewing, and pressing. If you slack off on the quality of any of these three components, you are likely to have problems matching seams. The narrow strips are the ones most likely to give you problems, so pay careful attention to these as they are cut, sewn, and pressed.

PROPORTIONS: I DIDN'T MEAN TO MAKE A TABLE RUNNER!

The instructions for the Divide and Conquer Convergence on page 42 begin with two squares. The interior of the final quilt is a long rectangular shape. If you wish, begin with vertical rectangles. Then the proportions won't be so extreme. See The Grand Convergence on pages 53 and 54 for additional information regarding proportions.

Finishing Touches

I get excited when my students reach the end of the Convergence quilt instructions and begin the creative process of deciding what to do next. The process of any Convergence quilt is working within a formula. The formula ends when the frames and borders begin. The quilts I chose for the galleries were selected first and foremost for the creative effort exhibited by the artist. Here are a few guidelines to help you through that creative part of completing your Convergence quilt.

THE NARROW FRAME

I often use a narrow frame to separate the interior of the quilt from the border. Narrow strips are hard to keep straight. Here are instructions for sewing a straight, narrow seam.

1. Cut the frame strip about 3/4" wide.
2. Place the strip on the quilt with right sides together. Check to make sure that the narrow strip is on top, wrong side up. Carefully match the edges and accurately sew using a narrow (approximately 1/4") seam.
3. Rather than pressing the seam toward the frame, press the seam toward the quilt top. You will soon see the advantage of pressing the seam toward the quilt. Sew on all four pieces. Press each frame toward the quilt.

BORDERS

1. This approach to adding borders is a bit different, so stay with me here! Position the quilt top wrong side up. Place the border strips underneath the quilt top, right sides together, matching the edges of the frame strip and border.
2. Now, instead of using the right side of the presser foot as a guide, use the *left* side of the presser foot as the guide. Butt the presser foot into the sewn seam.

Use the left edge of the presser foot along the seam.

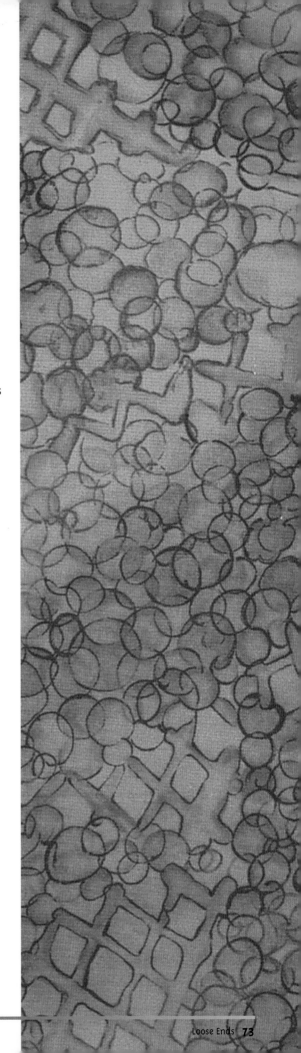

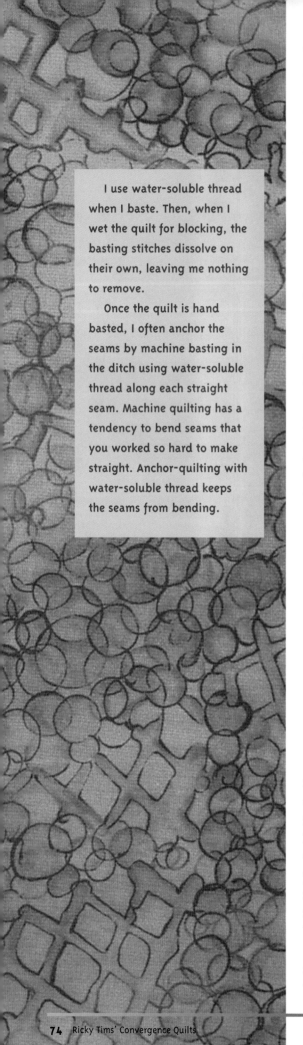

I use water-soluble thread when I baste. Then, when I wet the quilt for blocking, the basting stitches dissolve on their own, leaving me nothing to remove.

Once the quilt is hand basted, I often anchor the seams by machine basting in the ditch using water-soluble thread along each straight seam. Machine quilting has a tendency to bend seams that you worked so hard to make straight. Anchor-quilting with water-soluble thread keeps the seams from bending.

The presser foot will glide easily along the seam and create a perfectly straight frame. Better yet, by moving the needle position you can create smaller than $1/4$" frames. The seam allowance will be larger than a standard $1/4$", but it can be trimmed after the seam is sewn.

3. Finish the quilt top by adding other creative borders.

THE FINISH LINE

Batting Choice

My choice of batting is generally cotton. Cotton batting is rather "tacky" and helps prevent puckers. I use either 100% cotton batting or an 80/20 cotton/poly blend. One thing I do differently from a lot of quilters is that I don't trim the outside edges of my quilt before quilting it. Instead, I put together the quilt sandwich using an untrimmed quilt top.

Basting Method

I prefer to thread baste using the method described at left. Sometimes I use a light dusting of adhesive basting spray before thread basting my quilt. I prefer not to use safety pins for basting.

Quilting Designs

I enjoy machine quilting. When quilting a Convergence quilt, I prefer to use an overall design: one that enhances the quilt, has continuous quilting, and doesn't require marking. Here are three designs that are great for Convergence quilts. Shadow-trace the design with your finger or a pencil to "memorize," or become familiar with, the movement of each motif.

Continuous Teardrops   Flame Stitches   Circling Spirals

BLOCK IT

Before trimming and squaring my quilt, I soak it in the washing machine with cold water. It only soaks; it doesn't agitate. Then I use one spin cycle to remove most of the water. I put the quilt on a carpeted floor, and tug and pull the quilt until it is flat and square. I don't hesitate to use mats or rulers to insure that the quilt is not skewed. Once the quilt is dry, I use a ruler and rotary cutter to trim the edges in preparation for the binding. My edges are usually quilted heavily, but if you don't have a lot of quilting at the edge of your quilt, I would recommend using a wide and long zigzag stitch to secure the edges before adding the binding.

After I bind the quilt, it goes back into the washing machine, and I repeat the blocking process one more time. After the quilt dries, I add the sleeve, and the quilt will hang perfectly and beautifully flat.

Gallery: Author's Quilts

Tango by Ricky Tims, Arvada, Colorado, 60" x 57", 2002

Bolero by Ricky Tims, Arvada, Colorado, 60" x 50", 2002

Kimono Convergence (front) by Ricky Tims, Arvada, Colorado, garment, 2000

Kimono Convergence (back) by Ricky Tims, Arvada, Colorado, garment, 2000

Divide and Conquer: Awakening by Ricky Tims, Arvada, Colorado, 41" x 23", 1999

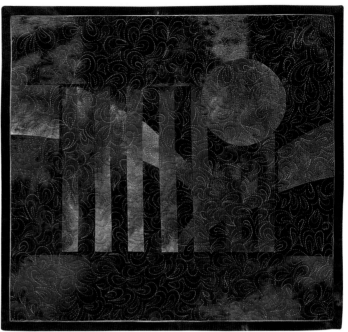

Sarabande by Ricky Tims, Arvada, Colorado, 19'' x 16'', 2002

Harmonic Convergence: Genesis by Ricky Tims, Arvada, Colorado, 32'' x 33'', 1999

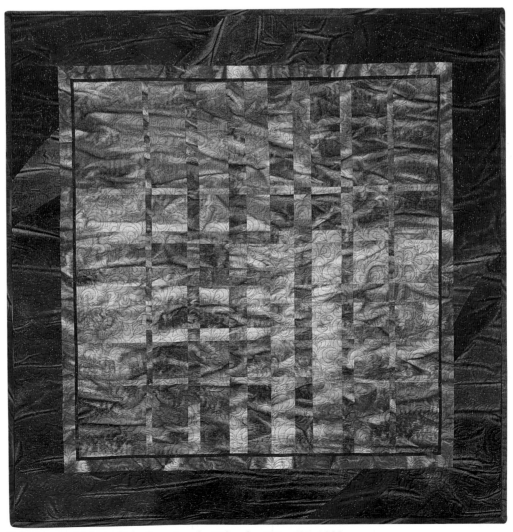

Reflections on Water by Ricky Tims, Arvada, Colorado, 42'' x 42'', 1999

Spirit of the Deep by Ricky Tims, Arvada, Colorado, 60" x 42", 2000

Dreamscape by Ricky Tims, Arvada, Colorado, 82" x 57", 2001

Index

About Ricky

Ricky Tims is known in the international world of quilting as an enthusiastic and encouraging teacher, an award-winning quilter, and a talented and spellbinding speaker. His innovative and entertaining presentations feature live music and humor combined with scholarly insights. His quilts have been displayed worldwide, and are highly regarded as excellent examples of contemporary quilts with traditional appeal. Ricky began designing and making quilts in 1991, and was recently selected as one of "The Thirty Most Distinguished Quilters in the World." He maintains an extensive international schedule of teaching and speaking engagements, and also he presents national seminars and the week-long Rocky Mountain Quilt Retreat in Colorado. Ricky is passionate about quilting, and is delighted to share his experience and enthusiasm with quilters at every level of expertise. He is challenged by creativity in all forms, and encourages individuals to cultivate self-expression, reach for the unreachable, and believe in the impossible.

Quilting is a relatively new interest compared to Ricky's lifelong passion for music. He began formal music lessons at the age of three. He is a conductor, composer, arranger, music producer, and performing artist. Ricky is proud to have implemented and conducted the 1998 concert "When We No Longer Touch" featuring the St. Louis Voices United Chorus and members of the St. Louis Symphony Orchestra. *Passage*, the CD recording of this unique concert, was released in December 1998. He has also produced several solo piano recordings. His blend of music and quilting is unique and remarkable. You can learn more about Ricky and order his fabrics at www.rickytims.com.

Other Fine Books by C&T Publishing

15 Two-Block Quilts: Unlock the Secrets of Secondary Patterns, Claudia Olson

24 Quilted Gems: Sparkling Traditional & Original Projects, Gai Perry

250 Continuous-Line Quilting Designs for Hand, Machine & Long-Arm Quilters, Laura Lee Fritz

250 More Continuous-Line Quilting Designs for Hand, Machine & Long-Arm Quilters, Laura Lee Fritz

All About Quilting from A to Z, From the Editors and Contributors of Quilter's Newsletter Magazine and Quiltmaker magazine

America from the Heart: Quilters Remember September 11, 2001, Karey Bresenhan

Appliqué 12 Easy Ways!: Charming Quilts, Giftable Projects, & Timeless Techniques, Elly Sienkiewicz

Appliqué Inside the Lines: 12 Quilt Projects to Embroider & Appliqué, Carol Armstrong

At Piece With Time: A Woman's Journey Stitched in Cloth, Kristin Steiner & Diane Frankenberger

Beautifully Quilted with Alex Anderson: · How to Choose or Create the Best Designs for Your Quilt · 6 Timeless Projects · Full-Size Patterns, Ready to Use, Alex Anderson

Cats in Quilts: 14 Purrfect Projects, Carol Armstrong

Celebrate the Tradition with C&T Publishing: Over 70 Fabulous New Blocks, Tips & Stories from Quilting's Best, C&T Staff

Contemporary Classics in Plaids & Stripes: 9 Projects from Piece 'O Cake Designs, Linda Jenkins & Becky Goldsmith

Cut-Loose Quilts: Stack, Slice, Switch, and Sew, Jan Mullen

Dresden Flower Garden: A New Twist on Two Quilt Classics, Blanche Young

Easy Pieces: Creative Color Play with Two Simple Quilt Blocks, Margaret Miller

Elm Creek Quilts: Quilt Projects Inspired by the Elm Creek Quilts Novels, Jennifer Chiaverini & Nancy Odom

Exploring Machine Trapunto: New Dimensions, Hari Walner

Fast, Fun & Easy Fabric Bowls: 5 Reversible Shapes to Use & Display, Linda Johanson

Felt Wee Folk: Enchanting Projects, Salley Mavor

Floral Affair, A: Quilts & Accessories for Romantics, Nihon Vogue

Flowering Favorites from Piece O' Cake Designs: Becky Goldsmith & Linda Jenkins

Free-Style Quilts: A "No Rules" Approach, Susan Carlson

Ghost Layers and Color Washes: Three Steps to Spectacular Quilts, Katie Pasquini Masopust

Heirloom Machine Quilting, Third Edition: Comprehensive Guide to Hand-Quilting Effects Using Your Sewing Machine, Harriet Hargrave

Hunter Star Quilts & Beyond: Jan Krentz

Liberated String Quilts, Gwen Marston

Lone Star Quilts and Beyond: Step-by-Step Projects and Inspiration, Jan Krentz

Luscious Landscapes: Simple Techniques for Dynamic Quilts, Joyce R. Becker

Make it Simpler Paper Piecing: Easy as 1-2-3 — A Pinless Fold & Sew Technique, Anita Grossman Solomon

Mary Mashuta's Confetti Quilts: A No-Fuss Approach to Color, Fabric & Design, Mary Mashuta

New Look at Log Cabin Quilts, A: Design a Scene Block by Block PLUS 10 Easy-to-Follow Projects, Flavin Glover

New Sampler Quilt, The, Diana Leone

On the Surface: Thread Embellishment & Fabric Manipulation, Wendy Hill

Paper Piecing Picnic: Fun-Filled Projects for Every Quilter, From the Editors and Contributors of Quilter's Newsletter Magazine and Quiltmaker magazine

Paper Piecing Potpourri: Fun-Filled Projects for Every Quilter, From the Editors and Contributors of Quilter's Newsletter Magazine and Quiltmaker magazine

Paper Piecing with Alex Anderson: ·Tips ·Techniques ·6 Projects, Alex Anderson

Piecing: Expanding the Basics, Ruth B. McDowell

Plentiful Possibilities: A Timeless Treasury of 16 Terrific Quilts, Lynda Milligan & Nancy Smith

Ultimate Guide to Longarm Quilting, The: ·How to Use Any Longarm Machine ·Techniques, Patterns & Pantographs ·Starting a Business ·Hiring a Longarm Machine Quilter, Linda Taylor

Radiant New York Beauties: 14 Paper-Pieced Quilt Projects, Valori Wells

Reverse Appliqué with No Brakez, Jan Mullen

Rotary Cutting with Alex Anderson: Tips, Techniques, and Projects, Alex Anderson

Shoreline Quilts: 15 Glorious Get-Away Projects, compiled by Cyndy Rymer

Show Me How to Machine Quilt: A Fun, No-Mark Approach, Kathy Sandbach

Simple Fabric Folding for Christmas: 14 Festive Quilts & Projects, Liz Aneloski

Skydyes: A Visual Guide to Fabric Painting, Mickey Lawler

Slice of Christmas from Piece O' Cake Designs, A, Linda Jenkins & Becky Goldsmith

Sweet Dreams, Moon Baby: A Quilt to Make, A Story to Read, Elly Sienkiewicz

Teddy Bear Redwork: ·25 Fresh, New Designs ·Step-by-Step Projects ·Quilts and More, Jan Rapacz

Wine Country Quilts: A Bounty of Flavorful Projects for Any Palette, Cyndy Lyle Rymer & Jennifer Rounds

When Quilters Gather: 20 Patterns of Piecers at Play, Ruth McDowell

Workshop with Velda Newman, A: Adding Dimension to Your Quilts, Velda E. Newman

For more information, write for a free catalog:
C&T Publishing, Inc.
P.O. Box 1456
Lafayette, CA 94549
800-284-1114
Email: ctinfo@ctpub.com
Website: www.ctpub.com

For quilting supplies:
Cotton Patch Mail Order
3405 Hall Lane, Dept.CTB
Lafayette, CA 94549
800-835-4418
925-283-7883
Email:quiltusa@yahoo.com

To order Ricky's hand-dyed fabrics go to:
www.rickytims.com

Note: Fabrics used in the quilts shown may not be currently available since fabric manufacturers keep most fabrics in print for only a short time.